Math Contests
for
High School
Volume 4

School Years: 1996-1997 through 2000-2001

Written by

Steven R. Conrad • Daniel Flegler

Published by MATH LEAGUE PRESS
Printed in the United States of America

Cover art by Bob DeRosa

Second Printing, 2008
Copyright © 2001, 2008
by Mathematics Leagues Inc.
All Rights Reserved

Math League Press
P.O. Box 17
Tenafly, NJ 07670-0017

ISBN 0-940805-14-6

Preface

Math Contests—High School, Volume 4 is the fourth volume in our series of problem books for high school students. The first three volumes contain contests given in the school years 1977-1978 through 1995-1996. Volume 5 contains the contests given in the school years 2001-2002 through 2005-2006. This volume contains contests given from 1996-1997 through 2000-2001. (Use the order form on page 70 to order any of our 15 books.)

These books give classes, clubs, teams, and individuals diversified collections of high school math problems. All of these contests were used in regional interscholastic competition throughout the United States and Canada. Each contest was taken by about 80 000 students. In the contest section, each page contains a complete contest that can be worked during a 30-minute period. The convenient format makes this book easy to use in a class, a math club, or for just plain fun. In addition, detailed solutions for each contest also appear on a single page.

Every contest has questions from different areas of mathematics. The goal is to encourage interest in mathematics through solving *worthwhile* problems. Many students first develop an interest in mathematics through problem-solving activities such as these contests. On each contest, the last two questions are generally more difficult than the first four. The final question on each contest is intended to challenge the very best mathematics students. The problems require no knowledge beyond secondary school mathematics. No knowledge of calculus is required to solve any of these problems. From two to four questions on each contest are accessible to students with only a knowledge of elementary algebra. Starting with the 1992-93 school year, students have been permitted to use any calculator without a QWERTY keyboard on any of our contests.

This book is divided into four sections for ease of use by both students and teachers. The first section of the book contains the contests. Each contest contains six questions that can be worked in a 30-minute period. The second section of the book contains detailed solutions to all the contests. Often, several solutions are given for a problem. Where appropriate, notes about interesting aspects of a problem are mentioned on the solutions page. The third section of the book consists of a listing of the answers to each contest question. The last section of the book contains the difficulty rating percentages for each question. These percentages (based on actual student performance on these contests) determine the relative difficulty of each question.

You may prefer to consult the answer section rather than the solution section when first reviewing a contest. The authors believe that reworking a problem, knowing the answer (but *not* the solution), often helps to better understand problem-solving techniques.

Revisions have been made to the wording of some problems for the sake of clarity and correctness. The authors welcome comments you may have about either the questions or the solutions. Though we believe there are no errors in this book, each of us agrees to blame the other should any errors be found!

Steven R. Conrad & Daniel Flegler, contest authors

Acknowledgments

For the beauty, cleverness, and breadth of his numerous mathematical contributions for the past 25 years, we are indebted to Michael Selby.

For her continued patience and understanding, special thanks to Marina Conrad, whose only mathematical skill, an important one, is the ability to count the ways.

For demonstrating the meaning of selflessness on a daily basis, special thanks to Grace Flegler.

To Daniel Will-Harris, whose skill in graphic design is exceeded only by his skill in writing *really* funny computer books, thanks for help when we needed it most: the year we first began to typeset these contests on a computer.

Table Of Contents

Preface i

Acknowledgements ii

School Year	Contest #	Page # for Problems	Page # for Solutions	Page # for Answers	Page # for Difficulty Ratings
1996-1997	1	2	34	66	68
1996-1997	2	3	35	66	68
1996-1997	3	4	36	66	68
1996-1997	4	5	37	66	68
1996-1997	5	6	38	66	68
1996-1997	6	7	39	66	68
1997-1998	1	8	40	66	68
1997-1998	2	9	41	66	68
1997-1998	3	10	42	66	68
1997-1998	4	11	43	66	68
1997-1998	5	12	44	66	68
1997-1998	6	13	45	66	68
1998-1999	1	14	46	66	68
1998-1999	2	15	47	66	68
1998-1999	3	16	48	66	68
1998-1999	4	17	49	66	68
1998-1999	5	18	50	66	68
1998-1999	6	19	51	66	68
1999-2000	1	20	52	67	68
1999-2000	2	21	53	67	68
1999-2000	3	22	54	67	68
1999-2000	4	23	55	67	68
1999-2000	5	24	56	67	68
1999-2000	6	25	57	67	68
2000-2001	1	26	58	67	68
2000-2001	2	27	59	67	68
2000-2001	3	28	60	67	68
2000-2001	4	29	61	67	68
2000-2001	5	30	62	67	68
	6	31	63	67	68

Order Form For Contest Books (Grades 4-12) 70

The Contests

October, 1996 – March, 2001

HIGH SCHOOL MATHEMATICS CONTESTS

Math League Press, P.O. Box 17, Tenafly, New Jersey 07670-0017

Contest Number 1   *Any calculator without a QWERTY keyboard is allowed.* Answers must be exact *or* have 4 (or more) significant digits, correctly rounded.   **October 22, 1996**

Name _____ Teacher _____ Grade Level ____ Score ____

Time Limit: 30 minutes   *Answer Column*

1-1. Ali is thinking of a whole number. When her number is divided by 99, the remainder is 8. What is the remainder when Ali's number is divided by 9?

1-1.

1-2. What is the only negative integer n which satisfies

$$n(n + 1)(n + 2)(n + 3) = 4 \times 3 \times 2 \times 1?$$

1-2.

1-3. Segments drawn from a vertex of a rectangle to points A and B on the longer side have lengths 25 and 39. If the shorter side of the rectangle has length 15, how long is $\overline{AB}$?

1-3.

1-4. If $x^2 + xy + y^2 = 7$ and $x + y = 2$, what is the value of xy?

1-4.

1-5. There are 5 positive integers less than 6, and 3 of these are factors of 6; so 60% of the positive integers less than 6 are factors of 6. What is the smallest positive integer $n > 1$ for which fewer than 1% of the positive integers **less than** n are factors of n?

1-5.

1-6. It can be proven that there are exactly three integral values of x for which $4^x + 4^{1993} + 4^{1996}$ is a perfect square (the square of an integer). What are these three values of x?

1-6.

HIGH SCHOOL MATHEMATICS CONTESTS

Math League Press, P.O. Box 17, Tenafly, New Jersey 07670-0017

Contest Number 2 *Any calculator without a QWERTY keyboard is allowed.* Answers must be exact *or* have 4 (or more) significant digits, correctly rounded. **November 19, 1996**

Name _____ Teacher _____ Grade Level _____ Score _____

Time Limit: 30 minutes | *Answer Column*

2-1. For what positive integer n does
$$n^2 \times 1995^2 \times 1996^2 \times 1997^2 = 3990^2 \times 3992^2 \times 3994^2?$$

2-1.

2-2. For what real number k is the equation $(10x + 5)^4 = k(2x + 1)^4$ an *identity* that is always true for every real number x?

2-2.

2-3. In the graph shown, one line segment passes through (0,5) and (4,0), and the other passes through (0,–2) and (1,0). What are the coordinates of the point of intersection of these two segments?

2-3.

2-4. What is the least integer n greater than 1 for which the square root of n, the cube root of n, and the fourth root of n are all integers?

2-4.

2-5. The *New York Times* crossword puzzle for August 25, 1995 had 225 cells arranged in 15 rows and 15 columns. Every cell was blank or held a letter for both a horizontal word and a vertical word. Horizontally, there were 10 three-letter words, 8 four-letter words, 8 five-letter words, 6 six-letter words, and some number of nine-letter words. Vertically, there were 4 three-letter words, 6 four-letter words, 6 five-letter words, 10 six-letter words, 2 seven-letter words, 4 eight-letter words, and some number of ten-letter words. How many cells were blank?

2-5.

2-6. What is the thousands' digit of 11^{86}?

2-6.

HIGH SCHOOL MATHEMATICS CONTESTS

Math League Press, P.O. Box 17, Tenafly, New Jersey 07670-0017

Contest Number 3 *Any calculator without a QWERTY keyboard is allowed.* Answers must be exact *or* have 4 (or more) significant digits, correctly rounded. **December 17, 1996**

Name _____ Teacher _____ Grade Level ____ Score ____

Time Limit: 30 minutes | *Answer Column*

3-1. In how many different ways can 10 be written as the sum of four (not necessarily different) positive *odd* integers? [NOTE: Sums which differ only in the order of addition are not counted as different.]

3-1.

3-2. Twenty externally tangent congruent circles are drawn as shown. The centers of three of these circles are the vertices of a right triangle, as illustrated. If the length of a radius of each of the 20 circles is 4, what is the perimeter of the right triangle?

3-2.

3-3. If $(a,1996)$ and $(1996,b)$ are different points on the graph of the line $y = \frac{3}{4}x + 5$, what is the value of $\frac{1996 - a}{1996 - b}$?

3-3.

3-4. From the top of a tree 36 m tall, the angle of elevation to the top of a second tree is 30°, while the angle of depression to the base of the second tree is 60°. How tall is the second tree, in m?

3-4.

3-5 [*An old, classic problem.*] Every day, at noon, a ship leaves Miami for Montreal, and another leaves Montreal for Miami. Each trip lasts 6 days, exactly 144 hours. How many Montreal-to-Miami ships will the ship leaving Miami today pass at sea (not at port) from the time it departs till the time it arrives in Montreal?

3-5.

3-6. Let ℓ_1 be the perimeter of the ellipse $\frac{x^2}{36} + \frac{y^2}{16} = 1$, and let ℓ_2 be the perimeter of the ellipse $\frac{x^2}{36} + \frac{y^2}{81} = 1$. What is the ratio of ℓ_1 to ℓ_2?

3-6.

© 1996 by Mathematics Leagues Inc.

4   Solutions on Page 36 • Answers on Page 66

Contest Number 4 *Any calculator without a QWERTY keyboard is allowed.* Answers must be exact *or* have 4 (or more) significant digits, correctly rounded. **January 14, 1997**

Name _____ **Teacher** _____ **Grade Level** _____ **Score** ____

Time Limit: 30 minutes

		Answer Column
4-1.	If $(x + 1)(x - 1) = 8$, what is the value of $(x^2 + x)(x^2 - x)$?	4-1.
4-2.	If a certain number is decreased by 7 and the difference is then multiplied by 7, the result is the same as when the number is decreased by 11 and that difference is multiplied by 11. What is this number?	4-2.
4-3.	A regular hexagon whose perimeter is 12 can be inscribed in a certain rectangle, as shown. What is the area of this rectangle?	4-3.
4-4.	If $\sin^2 x + \cos^2 x = \tan^2 x$, what is the value of $\sec^2 x$?	4-4.
4-5.	If $a = 17^{9x^{52} - 3x^9 - 1} + 17^{3x^9 - 9x^{52} + 1}$ and $b = 17^{9x^{52} - 3x^9 - 1} - 17^{3x^9 - 9x^{52} + 1}$, what is the value of $a^2 - b^2$ when $x = 1997$?	4-5.
4-6.	Jack and Jill each wrote a different whole number. Taken together, these numbers use only the digits 1 through 9 and use each digit exactly once. These numbers have the largest possible product for two such numbers. What is the larger of these two numbers? [NOTE: To clarify, the numbers might have been 195 and 478 362; but they aren't, since there is at least one pair of numbers meeting the conditions whose product is more than $195 \times 478\,362$.]	4-6.

HIGH SCHOOL MATHEMATICS CONTESTS

Math League Press, P.O. Box 17, Tenafly, New Jersey 07670-0017

Contest Number 5 *Any calculator without a QWERTY keyboard is allowed.* Answers must be exact *or* have 4 (or more) significant digits, correctly rounded. **February 11, 1997**

Name _____ Teacher _____ Grade Level ____ Score ____

Time Limit: 30 minutes   *Answer Column*

5-1.	As shown at the right, a line segment is drawn connecting the midpoints of two opposite sides of a rectangle. A diagonal of the rectangle is also drawn. If the area of each shaded triangle is 20, what is the area of the original rectangle?	5-1.
5-2.	How many digits are in the smallest positive integer whose digits have a sum of 1997?	5-2.
5-3.	Let $P(x) = x^3 + 6x^2 + 7x + 2$. What is the real number c for which the polynomial $P(x + c)$ has no x^2 term?	5-3.
5-4.	In discussing who was the best catcher, Marina said "Keith is best," Ali said "I'm not best," Keith said "Brian is best," and Brian said "Keith lied when he said I'm best." If one of these four statements is true, and the others are false, who is the best catcher?	5-4.
5-5.	In right triangle T, if we add the lengths of the legs, then square the sum, we'll get 1000. If we multiply the lengths instead, then square the product, we'll get 2500. How long is the hypotenuse of T?	5-5.
5-6.	What is the ordered pair of positive integers (a,b) for which $\frac{a}{b}$ is a reduced fraction and $x = \frac{a\pi}{b}$ is the least positive solution of $$(2\cos 8x - 1)(2\cos 4x - 1)(2\cos 2x - 1)(2\cos x - 1) = 1?$$	5-6.

© 1997 by Mathematics Leagues Inc.

HIGH SCHOOL MATHEMATICS CONTESTS

Math League Press, P.O. Box 17, Tenafly, New Jersey 07670-0017

Contest Number 6   *Any calculator without a QWERTY keyboard is allowed.* Answers must be exact *or* have 4 (or more) significant digits, correctly rounded.   **March 18, 1997**

Name _____ Teacher _____ Grade Level ____ Score ____

Time Limit: 30 minutes   *Answer Column*

6-1.   What is the real number c for which $\dfrac{-6 + \sqrt{36 - 4c}}{2} = 4$?

6-1.

6-2.   The solution sets of the polynomial equations $f(x) = 0$ and $g(x) = 0$ are, respectively, $\{0,1,2,3\}$ and $\{2,3,4\}$. How many different numbers are in the solution set of the polynomial equation

$$[f(x)][g(x)] = 0?$$

6-2.

6-3.   A rectangle is subdivided into 6 regions as shown in the picture at the right (which is *not* drawn to scale), In the picture, all the unshaded regions are squares. If the area of square A is 144, and the area of square B is 100, what is the area of the shaded region?

6-3.

6-4.   What are all values of x for which $\log_2(9 - 2^x) = 3 - x$?

6-4.

6-5.   I picked one of two coins at random, then tossed it three times. It landed heads up each time. If one coin was fair and the other two-headed, what is the probability that I picked the two-headed coin?

6-5.

6-6.   If a and b are positive integers, what is the smallest value of b for which

$$\frac{1995}{1996} < \frac{a}{b} < \frac{1996}{1997}?$$

6-6.

HIGH SCHOOL MATHEMATICS CONTESTS

Math League Press, P.O. Box 17, Tenafly, New Jersey 07670-0017

Contest Number 1 *Any calculator without a QWERTY keyboard is allowed.* Answers must be exact *or* have 4 (or more) significant digits, correctly rounded. **October 28, 1997**

Name _____ Teacher _____ Grade Level ____ Score ____

Time Limit: 30 minutes | *Answer Column*

1-1. It can be proven that $\sqrt{n^3 + 1}$ is an integer for only 3 integral values of n. What are these 3 values? | 1-1.

1-2. On a 100-question test, 60 questions involve algebra and 20 questions are difficult. If 8 of the difficult questions involve algebra, how many of the questions that are *not* difficult do *not* involve algebra? | 1-2.

1-3. In the rectangle that's illustrated at the right, $AB = 5$ and $BC = CD = 12$. How long is $\overline{AD}$? | 1-3.

1-4. A line the sum of whose x- and y-intercepts is 3 will be called a *3-line*. What is the sum of the y-intercepts of the two 3-lines that pass through the point $(-2,-4)$? | 1-4.

1-5. What is the sum of all the coefficients (including the constant term) in the polynomial expansion of
$$(x - 1)(x - 2)(x - 3)(x - 4) \times \ldots \times (x - 1996)(x - 1997)?$$ | 1-5.

1-6. If a *decreasing number* is a positive integer with two or more digits in which no two digits are alike and all are written in decreasing order from left to right, then how many decreasing numbers are there? | 1-6.

Solutions on Page 40 • Answers on Page 66

HIGH SCHOOL MATHEMATICS CONTESTS

Math League Press, P.O. Box 17, Tenafly, New Jersey 07670-0017

Contest Number 2 *Any calculator without a QWERTY keyboard is allowed.* Answers must be exact *or* have 4 (or more) significant digits, correctly rounded. **December 2, 1997**

Name _____ Teacher _____ Grade Level _____ Score _____

Time Limit: 30 minutes   *Answer Column*

2-1. Two positive integers will be called *reversible* if the digits of one of the integers, when written in reverse order, are the digits of the other integer. For example, 246 and 642 are reversible. What are two reversible numbers whose product is 564525?	2-1.
2-2. In square $ABCD$, $\overline{FE} \perp \overline{BD}$, as pictured at the right. If $BP = EF = 12$, what is BD?	2-2.
2-3. The *median* of $\{2^k, 2^{k+1}, 2^{k+2}, 2^{k+3}\}$ is the arithmetic mean of the two middle numbers. If k is a positive integer, what is the result, in simplest form, of dividing this median by the smallest of the four numbers?	2-3.
2-4. After my 16-digit credit card number was written below (one digit per box), some digits were erased. If the sum of the digits in any four consecutive boxes was 24, what was the sum of the seven digits between the two 9's shown?	2-4.
2-5. What is the least integral value of t for which the roots of the equation $x^2 + 2(t+1)x + 9t - 5 = 0$ are unequal negative numbers?	2-5.
2-6. The volume of one of four similar solids equals the sum of the volumes of the other three, and the surface areas of the solids are the squares of four consecutive integers. What is the surface area of the largest of these solids?	2-6.

For 2-4: `[ ][ ][1][9][ ][ ][ ][ ][ ][ ][9][7][ ][ ][ ]`

HIGH SCHOOL MATHEMATICS CONTESTS

Math League Press, P.O. Box 17, Tenafly, New Jersey 07670-0017

Contest Number 3 *Any calculator without a QWERTY keyboard is allowed.* Answers must be exact *or* have 4 (or more) significant digits, correctly rounded. **January 6, 1998**

Name _____ Teacher _____ Grade Level _____ Score _____

Time Limit: 30 minutes   *Answer Column*

3-1. In a sequence of ten positive numbers, every term from the second term on exceeds the term before it by a positive integer. If the eighth term is 19, what is the least possible value of the last term?

3-1.

3-2. Racing around a track for 1 hour, Flash went 20 laps while Speedy went 15. At these rates, in exactly how many minutes did Flash travel 1 more lap than Speedy?

3-2.

3-3. What is the least positive integer with no odd digits that is divisible by 9?

3-3.

3-4. If $x^{x^3} = 3$, what is the value of x? [NOTE: x^{x^3} means $x^{\left(x^3\right)}$.]

3-4.

3-5. Let $[x]$ represent the greatest integer $\leq x$. For example, $[2\frac{1}{2}] = 2$ and $[-\frac{1}{2}] = -1$. If a, b, c, and d are real numbers, then how many *different* integers can be represented by an expression of the form

$$[1a + 9b + 9c + 8d] - 1[a] - 9[b] - 9[c] - 8[d]?$$

3-5.

3-6. In the diagram at the right, what is the area of $\triangle ABD$?

3-6.

© 1998 by Mathematics Leagues Inc.

Contest Number 4 *Any calculator without a QWERTY keyboard is allowed.* Answers must be exact *or* have 4 (or more) significant digits, correctly rounded. **February 3, 1998**

Name _____ Teacher _____ Grade Level ____ Score ____

Time Limit: 30 minutes | *Answer Column*

4-1. If each of *ab* and *cd* separately represents any two-digit number from 00 to 98, what is *any one* ordered pair (*ab*, *cd*) that would make both of the following statements true?

Jack was born in 19*ab* and turns *cd* years old in 1998. Jill was born in 19*cd* and turns *ab* years old in 1998.

4-1.

4-2. What is the value of *p* for which $\sqrt{\frac{3}{8}}$ is *p*% of $\sqrt{6}$?

4-2.

4-3. A 6 by 8 rectangle and a 9 by 12 rectangle share a common vertex as shown, and all interior points of the smaller rectangle are also interior points of the larger rectangle. What is the distance between the centers of the two rectangles?

4-3.

4-4. If $i = \sqrt{-1}$, what is the smallest positive integer *n* that satisfies

$$(1 + i)^n = (1 - i)^n?$$

4-4.

4-5. What are the coordinates of the point *P* on the lower half of the graph of the ellipse $\frac{x^2}{4} + \frac{y^2}{9} = 1$ for which $\angle AOP$, determined by points *A*(2,0), *O*(0,0), and *P*, has a 60° measure?

4-5.

4-6. The sums 7+8 = 15, 4+5+6 = 15, and 1+2+3+4+5 = 15 show all possible ways in which 15 can be written as a sum of two or more consecutive positive integers. The product of the smallest numbers in all these sums is 7×4×1 = 28. If we wrote 100 in all possible ways as a sum of two or more consecutive positive integers, what would be the product of the smallest numbers in all these sums?

4-6.

Solutions on Page 43 • Answers on Page 66

HIGH SCHOOL MATHEMATICS CONTESTS

Math League Press, P.O. Box 17, Tenafly, New Jersey 07670-0017

Contest Number 5   *Any calculator without a QWERTY keyboard is allowed.* Answers must be exact *or* have 4 (or more) significant digits, correctly rounded.   **March 10, 1998**

Name _____ Teacher _____ Grade Level ____ Score ____

Time Limit: 30 minutes   *Answer Column*

5-1. What are both values of x that satisfy $$1x + 9x + 9x + 7x = 1x^2 + 9x^2 + 9x^2 + 8x^2?$$	5-1.
5-2. What is the largest prime factor of 143 000 000?	5-2.
5-3. By finding a gold nugget, a prospector is said to "strike it rich." If, on any given day, a prospector has probability $\frac{1}{8}$ of striking it rich, what is the probability that at least one of the prospectors Al and Barb strike it rich on a day they both mine for gold?	5-3.
5-4. What is the average of the numbers $\log_{12}3$, $\log_{12}6$, and $\log_{12}8$?	5-4.
5-5. In the diagram, $\overline{AE} \perp \overline{AB}$, $\overline{CD} \parallel \overline{AE}$, and $\overline{BC} \parallel \overline{DE}$. If $CD = 4$, $AB = 3$, and $AE = 5$, and the distance from $\overline{AE}$ to $\overline{CD}$ is 2, what is the area of pentagon $ABCDE$?	5-5.
5-6. In terms of x, what is the polynomial P of least degree, with integral coefficients, for which $P(\sqrt{3} + \sqrt{2}) = \sqrt{3} - \sqrt{2}$?	5-6.

HIGH SCHOOL MATHEMATICS CONTESTS

Math League Press, P.O. Box 17, Tenafly, New Jersey 07670-0017

Contest Number 6 *Any calculator without a QWERTY keyboard is allowed. Answers must be exact or have 4 (or more) significant digits, correctly rounded.* **April 7, 1998**

Name _____ Teacher _____ Grade Level ____ Score ____

Time Limit: 30 minutes | *Answer Column*

6-1. If a is an integer, and if both roots $x^2 + ax + 17 = 0$ are positive integers, what is the value of a? | 6-1.

6-2. What is the minimum value of $|x + y + z|$, given that $|x| = 1998$, $|y| = 1999$, and $|z| = 2000$? | 6-2.

6-3. All five sides of a *Pythagorean pentagon* have integral lengths, and the sum of the squares of the lengths of the four smallest sides is equal to the square of the length of the longest side. What is the least possible perimeter of a Pythagorean pentagon? | 6-3.

6-4. For all real numbers x, the function f is periodic, with $f(x+6) = f(x+10) = f(x)$. If $f(22) = 22$, what is the value of $f(44)$? | 6-4.

6-5. As shown at the right, two congruent circles are inscribed in a rectangle so that each is tangent to three sides of the rectangle and to the other circle. A third circle, smaller than the other two, is tangent to both congruent circles and one side of the rectangle. If the area of each congruent circle is 64π, what is the area of the small circle? | 6-5.

6-6. In $\triangle ABC$, $\tan A$, $\tan B$, and $\tan C$ have integral values and form an increasing arithmetic progression. What is the value of $(\tan A)(\tan C)$? | 6-6.

Solutions on Page 45 • Answers on Page 66

HIGH SCHOOL MATHEMATICS CONTESTS

Math League Press, P.O. Box 17, Tenafly, New Jersey 07670-0017

Contest Number 1 *Any calculator without a QWERTY keyboard is allowed.* Answers must be exact *or* have 4 (or more) significant digits, correctly rounded. **October 27, 1998**

Name _____ Teacher _____ Grade Level _____ Score _____

Time Limit: 30 minutes   *Answer Column*

1-1. In 4 talks, each at least 1 hour long, I spoke for a total of 5 hours. What was the maximum possible length of my longest talk, *in minutes*?	1-1.
1-2. Whenever the number 66 . . . 66, which consists of only 6's, has twice as many digits as the number 33 . . . 33, which consists of only 3's, the product (66 . . . 66)(33 . . . 33) does NOT contain the digit *d*. What are all five possible values of *d*?	1-2.
1-3. The line $2y - 3x = 12$ intersects the x-axis at A and the y-axis at B. For what value of $k > 0$ will a line through B intersect the x-axis at $C(k,0)$ so that the area of $\triangle ABC$ is 21?	1-3.
1-4. At 6 o'clock, the tip of a clock's hour hand was 23 cm from the tip of its minute hand. At 9 o'clock, this distance was only 17 cm. By how many cm does the minute hand's length exceed the hour hand's length?	1-4.
1-5. The roots (real and imaginary) of the equation $x^3 + 78x + 666 = 0$ are a, b, and c. What is the value of $a^3 + b^3 + c^3$?	1-5.
1-6. If the minimum number of "Friday the 13th's" that can occur in a calendar year is m and the maximum number of "Friday the 13th's" that can occur in a calendar year is M, what is the ordered pair (m,M)?	1-6.

Solutions on Page 46 • Answers on Page 66

HIGH SCHOOL MATHEMATICS CONTESTS

Math League Press, P.O. Box 17, Tenafly, New Jersey 07670-0017

Contest Number 2 *Any calculator without a QWERTY keyboard is allowed.* Answers must be exact *or* have 4 (or more) significant digits, correctly rounded. **December 1, 1998**

Name _____ Teacher _____ Grade Level _____ Score _____

Time Limit: 30 minutes   *Answer Column*

2-1. Triangle T is *not* equilateral. If every side of triangle T has an integral length, what is the least possible perimeter of triangle T?

2-1.

2-2. When choosing from a list of four different whole numbers, I can select three whose product is 74, and you can select three whose product is 54. What is the product of all four numbers?

2-2.

2-3. What is the only positive value of x that satisfies $x^3 + x^4 = x^5$?

2-3.

2-4. A, B, C, and D are the centers of four congruent circles, tangent to each other as shown. If $AC = BD = 12$, what is the area of one of the four circles?

2-4.

2-5. What are all values of x that satisfy $\sqrt{x^2 - 3x + 2} < x + 3$?

2-5.

2-6. The area of a triangle is 5. Two of its vertices are at $(1,2)$ and $(4,4)$. Its third vertex is on the x-axis. What are all possible coordinates of this third vertex?

2-6.

© 1998 by Mathematics Leagues Inc.

HIGH SCHOOL MATHEMATICS CONTESTS

Math League Press, P.O. Box 17, Tenafly, New Jersey 07670-0017

Contest Number 3 · *Any calculator without a QWERTY keyboard is allowed.* Answers must be exact *or* have 4 (or more) significant digits, correctly rounded. · **January 5, 1999**

Name _____ Teacher _____ Grade Level ____ Score ____

Time Limit: 30 minutes | *Answer Column*

3-1. Three squares are lined up horizontally, as shown. The area of the first square is 9, the area of the second square is 16, and the area of the third square is 25. How long is $\overline{AB}$?

3-1.

3-2. If a, b, and c are three different positive integers that satisfy

$$\left(\sqrt{a}\right)^4 + \left(\sqrt{b}\right)^4 = \left(\sqrt{c}\right)^4,$$

what is the least possible value of the sum $a + b + c$?

3-2.

3-3. Point P splits a diameter of a circle into segments of lengths 2 and 6. What is the shortest distance from the center of this circle to a chord through P that makes a 30° angle with the diameter, as shown?

3-3.

3-4. For what value of n does $3^{1998} + 9^{999} + 27^n = 3^{1999}$?

3-4.

3-5. What are both integers x for which all three of the expressions $\dfrac{x}{x-2}$, $\dfrac{x}{x-4}$, and $\dfrac{x}{x-6}$ have integral values?

3-5.

3-6. Rowing upstream, Pat dropped a hat into the river. Ten minutes later, when he realized the hat was missing, he turned around (with no loss of time), rowed downstream, and retrieved the hat 1 km downstream from where he had dropped it. If the river flows at a constant rate, and Pat rows at a constant rate (relative to the river), what is the river's rate, in km/hr?

3-6.

© 1999 by Mathematics Leagues Inc.

HIGH SCHOOL MATHEMATICS CONTESTS

Math League Press, P.O. Box 17, Tenafly, New Jersey 07670-0017

Contest Number 4   *Any calculator without a QWERTY keyboard is allowed.* Answers must be exact *or* have 4 (or more) significant digits, correctly rounded.   **February 2, 1999**

Name _____ Teacher _____ Grade Level _____ Score _____

Time Limit: 30 minutes   *Answer Column*

4-1.   For what value of x does $\sqrt{45} = \sqrt{5} + \sqrt{x}$?

4-1.

4-2.   On Monday, a college student spent 30% of his $\$D$ weekly pay. On Tuesday, he spent 60% of the remainder. If this left him with $1 less than the amount he spent on Monday, what is the value of D?

4-2.

4-3.   Write, in simplest form, the value of the quotient
$$\frac{19^{98} + (342)(19^{97})}{19^{99}}.$$

4-3.

4-4.   Four congruent circles are placed in a 4×4 square so that each is tangent to two sides of the square and to two of the other circles. A smaller fifth circle is drawn tangent to each of the other four circles, as shown. How long is a radius of the fifth circle?

4-4.

4-5.   What is the greatest possible value of a for which there is at least one real solution (x, y) to the system $x^2 + y^2 = 1$ and $x^2 y^2 = a$?

4-5.

4-6.   A hound was chasing a fox. Whenever the hound took 4 leaps, the fox took 5. If 3 hound leaps cover the same distance as 4 fox leaps, and the fox's head start was equal to 90 hound leaps, how many leaps did the hound need to catch the fox?

4-6.

HIGH SCHOOL MATHEMATICS CONTESTS

Math League Press, P.O. Box 17, Tenafly, New Jersey 07670-0017

Contest Number 5 *Any calculator without a QWERTY keyboard is allowed.* Answers must be exact *or* have 4 (or more) significant digits, correctly rounded. **March 9, 1999**

Name _____ Teacher _____ Grade Level ____ Score ____

Time Limit: 30 minutes | *Answer Column*

5-1. For what positive integer c is there only one ordered pair of positive integers (a,b) that satisfies $a + b = c$? | 5-1.

5-2. Three solid gold spherical balls, with respective diameters of 3, 4, and 5, are melted down and recast into a single solid gold spherical ball of diameter d. What is the value of d? | 5-2.

5-3. Some students stood evenly spaced in a circular formation. They counted off, starting at 1 and continuing by consecutive integers once around the circle, clockwise. How many students were there if the student furthest from student 19 was student 99? | 5-3.

5-4. If x is randomly chosen from the positive real numbers less than 10, what is the probability that $x + \frac{3}{x} \le 4$? | 5-4.

5-5. Both times that brackets appear in the expression below, let [x] represent the greatest integer less than or equal to x. For example, [4.9] = 4. If $n = 602\,975\,024\,681\,576\,789\,349\,125$, what is the value of

$$\left[\frac{n}{10^{\left[\log_{10} n\right]}}\right]?$$
| 5-5.

5-6. If the shaded sector of the circle shown has a perimeter of 28 cm and an area of 49 cm², what is the length, in centimeters, of the arc of this sector? | 5-6.

Contest Number 6 *Any calculator without a QWERTY keyboard is allowed.* Answers must be exact *or* have 4 (or more) significant digits, correctly rounded. **April 13, 1999**

Name _____ Teacher _____ Grade Level _____ Score _____

Time Limit: 30 minutes   *Answer Column*

6-1. In the addition problem shown, each asterisk (*) denotes a missing digit, and the *'s are not necessarily identical. What final four-digit sum will result from the proper restoration of the missing digits?

$$\begin{array}{r} 82* \\ 1*9 \\ 1*64 \\ \hline 1**9 \end{array}$$

6-1.

6-2. What is the least possible area of a rectangle whose sides and diagonals all have positive integral lengths?

6-2.

6-3. Five equilateral triangles are constructed on the sides of a regular pentagon, exterior to the pentagon. When the outer vertices of these triangles are connected, a larger regular pentagon results, as shown. If the length of a side of the small pentagon is 1, then the length of a side of the large pentagon is $2\cos x$. What is the degree-measure of the positive acute angle x?

6-3.

6-4. The roots of $x^2 - 3x - 3 = 0$ are r and s. What is the value of $r + s - 3rs$?

6-4.

6-5. Let f be a function defined on the positive numbers. Assume that $f(x)$ is always positive and that f has an inverse f^{-1}. If $f^{-1}(x) = \dfrac{1}{f(x)}$ for all $x > 0$, what is the value of $f(1)$?

6-5.

6-6. In any *increasing geometric sequence* (such as 2, 6, 18), you multiply by a fixed constant greater than 1 to go from any one term to the next. If such a sequence is 7 terms long, and if all 7 terms are integers between 200 and 3000, what is the largest number in the sequence?

6-6.

Solutions on Page 51 • Answers on Page 66

HIGH SCHOOL MATHEMATICS CONTESTS

Math League Press, P.O. Box 17, Tenafly, New Jersey 07670-0017

Contest Number 1 *Any calculator without a QWERTY keyboard is allowed.* Answers must be exact *or* have 4 (or more) significant digits, correctly rounded. **October 26, 1999**

Name _____ Teacher _____ Grade Level ____ Score ____

Time Limit: 30 minutes | *Answer Column*

1-1. When the digits of the two-digit number x are reversed, we obtain the number y. If $x \neq y$, what is the least possible value of $|x - y|$? | 1-1.

1-2. In the diagram at the right, which is *not* drawn to scale, squares are drawn on all sides of a right triangle as shown. If the areas of the squares drawn on the legs are 19 and 99, what is the area of the square drawn on the hypotenuse? | 1-2.

1-3. How many positive integers less than 100 can be written as the product of the first powers of two different primes? | 1-3.

1-4. If x and y are integers, what is the least x for which $\dfrac{1}{640} = \dfrac{x}{10^y}$? | 1-4.

1-5. At a classroom costume party, the average age of the b boys is g, and the average age of the g girls is b. If the average age of everyone at the party (all these boys and girls, plus their 42-year-old teacher) is $b+g$, what is the value of $b+g$? | 1-5.

1-6. When a small triangle is surrounded by 3 other small triangles, the result is called a *four-triangle*. (Of the 3 four-triangles in the diagram, one is shaded.) If the integers 1 through 9 are written in the 9 small triangles at the right, 1 per triangle, so the sum of the 4 integers in each four-triangle is the same, what is the least possible value of this sum? | 1-6.

HIGH SCHOOL MATHEMATICS CONTESTS

Math League Press, P.O. Box 17, Tenafly, New Jersey 07670-0017

Contest Number 2 *Any calculator without a QWERTY keyboard is allowed.* Answers must be exact *or* have 4 (or more) significant digits, correctly rounded. **November 30, 1999**

Name _____ Teacher _____ Grade Level ____ Score ____

Time Limit: 30 minutes　　　　　　　　　　　　　　　　　　　　　　*Answer Column*

2-1.　What is the ordered pair of integers (a,b), with $b > a > 0$, that satisfies

$$\sqrt{3^2 + 4^2} = a^2 + b^2?$$

2-1.

2-2.　When the integer n is divided by 7, the remainder is 5. What is the remainder when $2n$ is divided by 7?

2-2.

2-3.　A professional works twice as fast at a certain task as an amateur, and an apprentice takes twice as long as a professional. If, working together, 12 amateurs can complete the task in 1 day, how many apprentices would be needed to complete the same task in 1 day?

2-3.

2-4.　If $\dfrac{1}{a(b+1)} + \dfrac{1}{b(a+1)} = \dfrac{1}{(a+1)(b+1)}$, what is the value of $\dfrac{1}{a} + \dfrac{1}{b}$?

2-4.

2-5.　The square in the diagram at the right has a vertex on each coordinate axis, a vertex at (19,99), and a vertex at (x,y), as illustrated. What is the ordered pair (x,y)?

y
(19,99)
(x,y)
x

2-5.

2-6.　Write down all the integers from 1 through 60 to form the number

12345678910111213141516171819 20 . . . 49505152535455565758 5960.

Now delete 100 digits from this number. Do not rearrange the remaining digits. Call the resulting number n. What is the largest possible value of n? [NOTE: For this problem, your answer *must be exact*.]

2-6.

HIGH SCHOOL MATHEMATICS CONTESTS

Math League Press, P.O. Box 17, Tenafly, New Jersey 07670-0017

Contest Number 3 *Any calculator without a QWERTY keyboard is allowed.* Answers must be exact *or* have 4 (or more) significant digits, correctly rounded. **January 11, 2000**

Name _____ Teacher _____ Grade Level ____ Score ___

Time Limit: 30 minutes | *Answer Column*

3-1. If $\frac{a}{b} = \frac{2}{3}$, what is the value of $900a^2 - 400b^2$? | 3-1.

3-2. What is the least possible area of a rectangle whose perimeter is 18 and each of whose sides has a positive integral length? | 3-2.

3-3. What is the units' digit of the sum of the squares of the first 2000 odd positive integers? | 3-3.

3-4. From a set of 9 cards numbered consecutively from 1 to 9, two cards (numbered x and y) are chosen at random, with replacement. What is the probability that x is less than y? | 3-4.

3-5. What is the largest value of x less than 1 for which $\frac{2}{x}$ is an integer? | 3-5.

3-6. As shown, semicircles are drawn on two adjacent sides of a square, interior to the square. If the length of a side of the square is 2, what is the length of a radius of the circle which is tangent, as shown, to both of the semicircles and the other two sides of the square? | 3-6.

© 2000 by Mathematics Leagues Inc.

22 Solutions on Page 54 • Answers on Page 67

HIGH SCHOOL MATHEMATICS CONTESTS

Math League Press, P.O. Box 17, Tenafly, New Jersey 07670-0017

Contest Number 4 *Any calculator without a QWERTY keyboard is allowed.* Answers must be exact *or* have 4 (or more) significant digits, correctly rounded. **February 8, 2000**

Name _____ Teacher _____ Grade Level ____ Score ____

Time Limit: 30 minutes   *Answer Column*

4-1. If Ali wrote a list of 2000 consecutive odd integers, by how much would the greatest number on her list exceed the smallest?	4-1.
4-2. I have three packages whose total weight is 60 kg. If the two heaviest packages weigh 50 kg together, and the two lightest weigh 25 kg together, what is the weight, in kg, of the heaviest package?	4-2.
4-3. The points (10,0), (0,0), and (0,4) are three vertices of the rectangle shown. For exactly two values of x, segments drawn from $(x,4)$ to (0,0) and (10,0) are perpendicular. One of these values is $x = 2$. What is the other?	4-3.
4-4. What is the ordered triple of positive integers (a,b,c), with a as small as possible, for which $|ax + b| \le c$ is equivalent to $-\frac{10}{3} \le x \le 1$?	4-4.
4-5. A smooth, round, cylindrical log, 17.5 m long and 0.5 m in diameter, rolled at a fixed velocity† across a flat rectangular field, always parallel to one side of the field. Just as the log entered the field, a squirrel jumped on at one end. The squirrel ran at a fixed velocity along the top of the moving log and jumped off the other end just when the log had rolled 60 m. How far, in m, had the squirrel run? † Velocity is a vector, so direction and speed are both fixed whenever the velocity is fixed.	4-5.
4-6. One real root of $x^4 - 14x^3 + 72x^2 - 162x + 133 = 0$ is between 2 and 3, the other is between 5 and 6, and the imaginary roots are $a \pm bi$, where a and b are non-zero real numbers. What is the integer nearest to a?	4-6.

Solutions on Page 55 • Answers on Page 67

HIGH SCHOOL MATHEMATICS CONTESTS

Math League Press, P.O. Box 17, Tenafly, New Jersey 07670-0017

Contest Number 5 *Any calculator without a QWERTY keyboard is allowed.* Answers must be exact *or* have 4 (or more) significant digits, correctly rounded. **March 7, 2000**

Name _____ Teacher _____ Grade Level ____ Score ____

Time Limit: 30 minutes   *Answer Column*

5-1. A line segment is drawn from one vertex of a square, through the midpoint of
a side, to an extension of another side,
as shown. If the area of the square is 64,
what is the area of the shaded triangle?

5-1.

5-2. For what prime number p is 15 a root of $x^2 - 5px + 6p^2 = 0$?

5-2.

5-3. Between 1 and 200, there is a sequence of 13 consecutive integers, none of which is a prime. What is the smallest of these integers?

5-3.

5-4. If $x^2 + x - 1 = 0$, what is the value of $x^4 + 2x^3 + x^2$?

5-4.

5-5. What are all degree-measures θ in the interval $0° \leq \theta < 360°$ that satisfy $\cos 4\theta + 3\cos 2\theta + 2 = 0$?

5-5.

5-6. For the set $\{a,b,c,d\}$, the sum of the products of the elements taken 2 at a time is
$ab + ac + ad + bc + bd + cd$; and the sum
of the products of the elements taken 3 at
a time is $abc + abd + acd + bcd$. Let $f(n)$
be the sum of the products of the first
2000 positive integers, taken n at a time.
For example, $f(1) =$ the sum of the first
2000 positive integers, and $f(2) =$ the sum
of the products of the first 2000 positive
integers, taken two at a time, etc. What is
the value of

$$f(1) + f(2) + f(3) + \ldots + f(1999) + f(2000)?$$

5-6.

HIGH SCHOOL MATHEMATICS CONTESTS

Math League Press, P.O. Box 17, Tenafly, New Jersey 07670-0017

Contest Number 6 *Any calculator without a QWERTY keyboard is allowed.* Answers must be exact *or* have 4 (or more) significant digits, correctly rounded. **April 11, 2000**

Name _____ Teacher _____ Grade Level ____ Score ____

Time Limit: 30 minutes | *Answer Column*

6-1. A square board has alternating dark and light squares, just like a checkerboard, except that there are 9 squares on each side (instead of 8). At most how many of the squares on this 9×9 board are dark?

6-1.

6-2. If n is an integer, what is the largest value of n that satisfies

$$(\pi - 1)(\pi - 2)(\pi - 3)(\pi - 4)(n) > 0?$$

6-2.

6-3. I bought two books for a total cost of $40. If the first book's price were raised 5% and the second's lowered 5%, the prices would be equal. What was the original price, in dollars, of the cheaper book?

6-3.

6-4. What is the only real number k for which there is no common solution to the pair of equations $998x + 999y = 1999$ and $1996x + ky = 2000$?

6-4.

6-5. What is the circumference of the circle circumscribed about an isosceles triangle whose legs are each 10 and whose base is 12?

6-5.

6-6. For what number k can the graph of $y = \frac{x-3}{1-3x}$ be transformed into the graph of $xy = k$ by a translation? [NOTE: If a *translation* moves every point a units horizontally and b units vertically, then the translation transforms the point (x,y) into the point $(x+a, y+b)$.]

6-6.

Solutions on Page 57 • Answers on Page 67

25

HIGH SCHOOL MATHEMATICS CONTESTS

Math League Press, P.O. Box 17, Tenafly, New Jersey 07670-0017

Contest Number 1 *Any calculator without a QWERTY keyboard is allowed.* Answers must be exact *or* have 4 (or more) significant digits, correctly rounded. **October 17, 2000**

Name _____ Teacher _____ Grade Level ____ Score ____

Time Limit: 30 minutes   *Answer Column*

1-1.	What are three different positive integers whose sum equals the product of the largest two of them?	1-1.
1-2.	What is the only prime $p > 0$ for which some integer n satisfies $\frac{p^2}{14} = \frac{n}{2}$?	1-2.
1-3.	A square is divided into twelve congruent rectangles, as shown. If the length of a diagonal of one of these rectangles is 5, what is the area of the square?	1-3.
1-4.	For unequal integers x and y, the expression $3x + 8y$ takes on a range of different integral values. For example, if $x = 1$ and $y = -1$, the value of $3x + 8y$ is -5. In this manner, what is the smallest positive integral value of $3x + 8y$?	1-4.
1-5.	The set $\mathbf{S} = \left\{ \frac{1}{15}, \frac{2}{15}, \frac{4}{15}, \frac{7}{15}, \frac{8}{15}, \frac{11}{15}, \frac{13}{15}, \frac{14}{15}, \ldots, \frac{74}{15} \right\}$ consists of every positive fraction whose denominator is 15, whose numerator is at most 74, and whose numerator and denominator are integers with a greatest common factor of 1. What is the sum of all the elements of $\mathbf{S}$?	1-5.
1-6.	With each entry I submit, I have to write a different pair of positive integers whose greatest common factor is 1 and whose sum is 2000. (Pairs differing only in the order of addition are counted as 1 pair, *not* as 2 different pairs.) For example, I submitted the pair (1, 1999) with my first entry. With these restrictions, at most how many entries can one person submit?	1-6.

HIGH SCHOOL MATHEMATICS CONTESTS

Math League Press, P.O. Box 17, Tenafly, New Jersey 07670-0017

Contest Number 2 *Any calculator without a QWERTY keyboard is allowed.* Answers must be exact *or* have 4 (or more) significant digits, correctly rounded. **November 14, 2000**

Name _____ Teacher _____ Grade Level ____ Score ___

Time Limit: 30 minutes	*Answer Column*
2-1. If n is a positive integer, what is the largest possible value of $$\frac{1}{n^2} + \frac{1}{(n+1)^2} + \frac{1}{(n+2)^2}?$$	2-1.
2-2. Which is larger, 2^{3000} or 3^{2000}?	2-2.
2-3. In a certain circle, the numerical sum of the area and circumference is 360π. How long is a radius of this circle?	2-3.
2-4. What is the smallest positive integer that leaves a remainder of 10 when divided into 200?	2-4.
2-5. Lines with slopes –1 and –2 are drawn through the first quadrant point (a,b), as shown, forming one triangle with a side on the x–axis and one triangle with a side on the y–axis. What is the total area of the two (shaded) triangles? (Write your answer explicitly in terms of a and b.)	2-5.
2-6. Working alone, Holmes puts two coats of paint on a wall, one before and one after lunch. One day, Holmes began at the usual time. Two hours before lunch he was joined by Watson, who paints at the rate of 600 m² each workday, and who left when the 1st coat was finished. Holmes promptly began the 2nd coat and had lunch at the usual time. One hour before his normal quitting time, Holmes had painted a 2nd coat everywhere except where Watson had painted that morning. If each man's normal workday is the same, and if each works at a constant rate, what was the area of the wall, in m²?	2-6.

Solutions on Page 59 • Answers on Page 67

HIGH SCHOOL MATHEMATICS CONTESTS

Math League Press, P.O. Box 17, Tenafly, New Jersey 07670-0017

Contest Number 3 *Any calculator without a QWERTY keyboard is allowed.* Answers must be exact *or* have 4 (or more) significant digits, correctly rounded. **December 12, 2000**

Name _____ Teacher _____ Grade Level _____ Score _____

Time Limit: 30 minutes | *Answer Column*

3-1. What is the only number x that satisfies $x^2 = x^4$, but *not* $x = x^2$? | 3-1.

3-2. What is the smallest positive integer that is *not* a factor of
$1\times2\times3\times4\times5\times6\times7\times8\times9\times10\times11\times12\times13\times14\times15\times16\times17\times18\times19\times20$? | 3-2.

3-3. Three congruent circles are tangent to each other as shown. What is the area of the circumscribing rectangle if its diagonal is 20? | 3-3.

3-4. My physics class learned how to fold a quadrilateral into a paper plane. As seen at the right, the lesson was successful. My quadrilateral's vertices were at (0,1), (0,0), (1,0), and (2000,2001). What was my quadrilateral's area? | 3-4.

3-5. What are both ordered pairs of integers (x,y) that satisfy
$$(1 + x + y)^2 = 1^2 + x^2 + y^2?$$ | 3-5.

3-6. Evaluate $\left(\frac{1}{2^2}+\frac{1}{3^2}+\frac{1}{4^2}+\ldots\right)+\left(\frac{1}{2^3}+\frac{1}{3^3}+\frac{1}{4^3}+\ldots\right)+\left(\frac{1}{2^4}+\frac{1}{3^4}+\frac{1}{4^4}+\ldots\right)+\ldots.$ | 3-6.

More formally, what is the sum of all fractions of the form $\dfrac{1}{(m+1)^{n+1}}$, where m and n range over the positive integers?

© 2000 by Mathematics Leagues Inc.

Solutions on Page 60 • Answers on Page 67

HIGH SCHOOL MATHEMATICS CONTESTS

Math League Press, P.O. Box 17, Tenafly, New Jersey 07670-0017

Contest Number 4 *Any calculator without a QWERTY keyboard is allowed. Answers must be exact or have 4 (or more) significant digits, correctly rounded.* **January 16, 2001**

Name _____ Teacher _____ Grade Level _____ Score ____

Time Limit: 30 minutes   *Answer Column*

4-1. The first number in a certain sequence is 12. From then on, each new number of the sequence equals the sum of the digits of the square of the previous number. For example, the second number is 9, since the sum of the digits of $12^2 = 144$ is 9. What is the 2001st number of this sequence?

4-1.

4-2. If $2^{10} + 4^{10}$ is written as the product of two consecutive positive integers, what is the smaller of these two consecutive integers?

4-2.

4-3. Since 1987, the population of Megalopolis has increased by 10%, while the number of taxicabs has decreased by 12%. By what per cent should the present number of taxicabs be increased to restore, to its 1987 level, the ratio of population to the number of taxicabs?

4-3.

4-4. The expression $D = \begin{vmatrix} r & s \\ t & u \end{vmatrix} = ru - st$ is called a *determinant*. Independently, each of the numbers r, s, t, and u is randomly assigned the value 0 or 1. What is the probability that D has a negative value?

4-4

4-5. What are the coordinates of the point on the graph of $x^2 + y^2 = 1$ that is nearest to (3,4)?

4-5.

4-6. What is the area of a circle in which the lengths of consecutive sides of an inscribed hexagon are 1, 1, 1, 2, 2, and 2?

4-6.

Contest Number 5 *Any calculator without a QWERTY keyboard is allowed.* Answers must be exact *or* have 4 (or more) significant digits, correctly rounded. **February 13, 2001**

Name _____ Teacher _____ Grade Level ____ Score ____

Time Limit: 30 minutes | *Answer Column*

5-1. If $x = \sqrt{2000}$ and $y = \sqrt{2001}$, what is the simplified numerical value of $(x + y)^2 + (x - y)^2$?

5-1.

5-2. For positive integers N, define $[]N[]$ by the following equations:

$$[]N[] = 2 + 4 + 6 + \ldots + N, \text{ if } N \text{ is even, and}$$
$$[]N[] = 1 + 3 + 5 + \ldots + N, \text{ if } N \text{ is odd.}$$

Two examples are: $[]8[] = 2 + 4 + 6 + 8 = 20$; and $[]9[] = 1 + 3 + 5 + 7 + 9 = 25$. What is the value of $[]2001[] - []2000[]$?

5-2.

5-3. A quadrilateral has two pairs of congruent sides and a longer diagonal of length 6, as shown. For what value of x will the area of the shaded region be 40% of the area of the unshaded region?

x $6-x$

5-3.

5-4. What are all ordered pairs of real numbers (x,y) for which

$$\frac{2}{x} + \frac{y}{3} = 3 \text{ and } \frac{x}{2} + \frac{3}{y} = \frac{3}{2}?$$

5-4.

5-5. What is the smallest number greater than 1 whose decimal representation differs from the decimal representation of its reciprocal only in the location of the decimal point?

5-5.

5-6. What are *both* complex numbers z for which $z^n = 1$ and $(z+1)^n = 1$ are both satisfied for the same positive integer n?

5-6.

HIGH SCHOOL MATHEMATICS CONTESTS

Math League Press, P.O. Box 17, Tenafly, New Jersey 07670-0017

Contest Number 6 *Any calculator without a QWERTY keyboard is allowed.* Answers must be exact *or* have 4 (or more) significant digits, correctly rounded. **March 20, 2001**

Name _____ Teacher _____ Grade Level _____ Score _____

Time Limit: 30 minutes | *Answer Column*

6-1. What is the least positive integer $n > 12$ for which $\sqrt{3n}$ is an integer? | 6-1.

6-2. For what value of n does $\left(1+\frac{1}{n}\right)\left(1+\frac{1}{n+1}\right)\left(1+\frac{1}{n+2}\right)\left(1+\frac{1}{n+3}\right) = \frac{51}{49}$? | 6-2.

6-3. Divide 360° into 100 congruent parts, each called a centigree. Divide each centigree into 10 congruent parts, each called a milligree. Using these measurements, $54°54' = c$ centigrees and m milligrees, where c is an integer and $0 \le m < 10$. What is the ordered pair (c,m)? | 6-3.

6-4. Two externally tangent circles are congruent. A line segment is drawn from the center of one circle, tangent to the other. If the length of this segment is 12, what is the area of the shaded region, as shown, which is bounded by the part of the line segment outside the two circles and an arc from each of the two circles? | 6-4.

6-5. Using my birdscissors, I cut $\triangle ABC$ out of a big piece of paper. I then took some measurements and found that $\sin A + \sin B + \sin C = \frac{5}{2}$ and $\frac{a}{\sin A} = 16$. What is the perimeter of the triangle I cut out? | 6-5.

6-6. What are all values of t for which the inequality

$$\frac{x^2 - tx - 2}{x^2 - 3x + 4} > -1$$

is satisfied for all real values of x? | 6-6.

Solutions on Page 63 • Answers on Page 67 31

Complete Solutions

· ·

October, 1996 – March, 2001

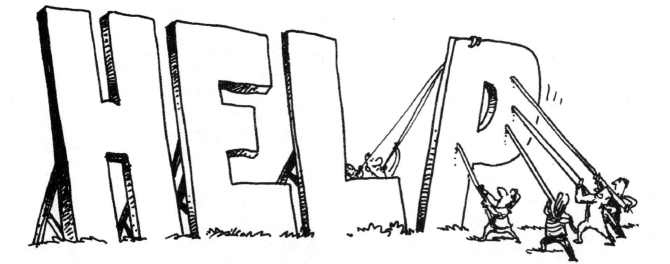

Problem 1-1

Method I: Since Ali's number is 8 more than a multiple of 99, Ali's number is of the form $99k+8$, where k is an integer. For $k = 1$, Ali's number is 107. When 107 is divided by 9, the remainder is $\boxed{8}$.

Method II: Ali's number is 8 more than a multiple of 99. Since 99 is itself a multiple of 9, Ali's number is also 8 more than a multiple of 9. Therefore, when Ali's number is divided by 9, the remainder is 8.

Problem 1-2

Method I: $n(n+1)(n+2)(n+3) = 4\times3\times2\times1 = (-4)(-3)(-2)(-1)$, so $n = 1$ or $n = \boxed{-4}$.

Method II: Graph $y = x(x+1)(x+2)(x+3) - 24$ on a graphing calculator. The graph crosses the x-axis only at $x = 1$ and $x = -4$.

Method III: Expanding, $n^4+6n^3+11n^2+6n = 24$. This equation has two real roots and two imaginary roots. The real roots are $n = 1$ and $n = -4$.

Problem 1-3

The width of the rectangle is 15, so right $\triangle DEA$ and right $\triangle DEB$ each have a leg of length 15. By the Pythagorean Theorem, $EA = 20$ and $EB = 36$. Finally $AB = EB - EA = 36 - 20 = \boxed{16}$.

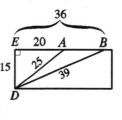

Problem 1-4

Method I: Since $x+y = 2$, $(x+y)^2 = x^2+2xy+y^2 = 2^2 = 4$. From this, subtract $x^2+xy+y^2 = 7$. The result is $xy = \boxed{-3}$.

Method II: $7 = x^2+xy+y^2 = (x+y)^2-xy = 2^2-xy = 4-xy$, so $xy = -3$.

Method III: If $y = -x+2$, then $x^2+xy+y^2 = 7$ becomes $x^2+x(2-x)+(2-x)^2 = 7$. When we simplify, we get $x^2-2x-3 = (x-3)(x+1) = 0$, so $(x,y) = (-1,3)$ or $(3,-1)$. Now, $xy = -3$.

Problem 1-5

Method I: Since fewer than 1% of the positive integers less than n are factors of n, there must be *more than* 100 numbers less than n that are not factors of n, so $n > 101$. By inspection, the answer is $\boxed{103}$.

Method II: If n is a prime, then 1 is the only positive integer less than n that's also a factor of n. If $1 < 1\%$ of the positive integers **less than** n, then $1 < \frac{n-1}{100}$; so $n > 101$. The least prime > 101 is 103.

Problem 1-6

Method I: Since $a^2+2ab+b^2 = (a+b)^2$, if the middle term of a trinomial equals twice the product of the square roots of the other two terms, the trinomial is the square of a binomial, so the trinomial is a perfect square. In this problem, it's easiest to write the middle term as twice the product of the square roots of the other terms if we first write each term as a power of 2; so rewrite $4^x + 4^{1993} + 4^{1996}$ as $2^{2x} + 2^{3986} + 2^{3992}$. There are three different terms. Since each can be "the middle term," we can write three equations that say that the middle term equals twice the product of the square roots of the other two terms. If 2^{3986} is the middle term, then $2^{3986} = 2(2^x)(2^{1996}) = 2^{1997+x}$, so $3986 = x + 1997$, and $x = 1989$. But if 2^{2x} is the middle term, then $2^{2x} = 2(2^{1993})(2^{1996}) = 2^{3990}$, so $2x = 3990$, and $x = 1995$. Finally, if 2^{3992} is the middle term, then $2^{3992} = 2(2^x)(2^{1993})$, so $3992 = x + 1994$, and $x = 1998$; and $4^x + 4^{1993} + 4^{1996}$ is a perfect square for these values of x: $\boxed{1989, 1995, 1998}$.

Method II: Factor out 4^{1988}, a perfect square. When is the other factor a perfect square? On a calculator with a table feature, set $y_1 = \sqrt{4^{x-1988} + 4^5 + 4^8}$, set TblMin = 1988, and set ΔTbl = 1. In the table, y_1 is integral at $x = 1989, 1995,$ and 1998.

Problem 2-1

Dividing both sides by $1995^2 \times 1996^2 \times 1997^2$, we get $n^2 = 2^2 \times 2^2 \times 2^2$. Since $n > 0$, $n = \boxed{8}$.

Problem 2-2

Method I: Since the equation is true for *every* real value of x, substitute $x = 0$ to get $k = 5^4$ or $\boxed{625}$.

Method II: Since $(10x + 5)^4 = [5(2x + 1)]^4 = 5^4(2x + 1)^4 = 625(2x + 1)^4$, the value of k is 625.

Problem 2-3

The lines have equations $y = 2x - 2$ and $y = -\frac{5}{4}x + 5$, so the lines intersect where $2x - 2 = -\frac{5}{4}x + 5$. The point of intersection is $\boxed{\left(\frac{28}{13}, \frac{30}{13}\right)}$.

Problem 2-4

Since n is a perfect square, cube, and fourth power, and since $n > 1$, we conclude that the least such integral $n = 2^x$, where x is the least common multiple of 2, 3, and 4; so $x = 12$ and $n = 2^{12} = \boxed{4096}$.

Problem 2-5

Method I: The number of cells used horizontally equals the number of cells used vertically. If H equals the number of horizontal 9-letter words, there are $3 \times 10 + 4 \times 8 + 5 \times 8 + 6 \times 6 + 9H = 138 + 9H$ horizontal cells used. The total number of cells is 225, so $H \leq 9$. If V is the number of vertical 10-letter words, there are $3 \times 4 + 4 \times 6 + 5 \times 6 + 6 \times 10 + 7 \times 2 + 8 \times 4 + 10V = 172 + 10V$ vertical cells used. Since the total number of cells is 225, $V \leq 5$. Since $138 + 9H = 172 + 10V$, we get $9H - 10V = 34$. Since $H \leq 9$ and $V \leq 5$, the only non-negative integral solution of this equation is

$(H,V) = (6,2)$. Since the total number of horizontal cells is $138 + 9H = 192$, the number of blank cells is $225 - 192 = \boxed{33}$.

Method II: Horizontally, 138 cells are already filled with letters. Therefore, $225 - 138 = 87$ cells are filled with either blanks or letters used in nine-letter words. If H is the number of horizontal nine-letter words and B is the number of blanks, then $9H + B = 87$. Also, since H is a non-negative integer, $0 \leq H \leq 9$. Vertically, 172 cells are already filled with letters. Therefore, $225 - 172 = 53$ cells are filled with either blanks or letters used in ten-letter words. If V is the number of vertical ten-letter words, then $10V + B = 53$. Also, V is a non-negative integer, so $0 \leq V \leq 5$. Subtracting $10V + B = 53$ from $9H + B = 87$, we get $9H - 10V = 34$. The only integral solution of this equation for which $0 \leq H \leq 9$ and $0 \leq V \leq 5$ is $(H,V) = (6,2)$. Substituting, $B = 33$.

Problem 2-6

Method I: Use a calculator, but don't use too many digits or you'll exceed the calculator's display capability. Use only the last four digits of each result to get the next result. That way, you'll keep track of the thousands' digit. (If you know number theory, we're computing in mod 10 000.) Let "$\equiv$" mean "has the same 4-digit ending as." Begin with $11^5 \equiv 1051$; Then, $11^{10} \equiv 1051^2 \equiv 4601$; $11^{20} \equiv 4601^2 \equiv 9201$; $11^{40} \equiv 9201^2 \equiv 8401$; $11^{80} \equiv 8401^2 \equiv 6801$; and $11^{85} \equiv 6801 \times 11^5 \equiv 6801 \times 1051 \equiv 7851$. Finally, $11^{86} \equiv 7851 \times 11 \equiv 6361$, whose thousands' digit is $\boxed{6}$.

Method II: Expand $N = 11^{86} = (1 + 10)^{86}$ by the Binomial Thm: $N = 1 + \binom{86}{1}(10) + \binom{86}{2}(10^2) + \binom{86}{3}(10^3) = 1 + 860 + 365500 + 102340(10^3) +$ terms containing a factor of 10^4. By adding together the first three terms, $N = 366361 +$ terms containing a factor of 10^4. Since these other terms have no effect on the thousands' digit, that digit is a 6.

Contests written and compiled by Steven R. Conrad & Daniel Flegler   Mathematics Leagues Inc., © 1996

Problem 3-1

Using just one 1, there's only one way: $1+3+3+3$.
Using just two 1's, there's only one way: $1+1+3+5$.
Using just three 1's, there's only one way: $1+1+1+7$.
All together, the number of ways is $\boxed{3}$.

Problem 3-2

The shorter leg consists of two diameters plus two radii, so it's as long as 6 radii. Likewise, the longer leg is as long as 8 radii. Therefore the hypotenuse is as long as 10 radii, and

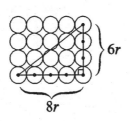

the triangle's perimeter is as long as 24 radii. Since the length of each radius is 4, the perimeter is $\boxed{96}$.

Problem 3-3

The slope of the line is $\dfrac{b-1996}{1996-a}$, which equals $\dfrac{3}{4}$. We're asked for $\dfrac{1996-a}{1996-b}$, which is the negative reciprocal of the given slope. Its value is $\boxed{-\dfrac{4}{3}}$.

Problem 3-4

As shown at the right, there are several different 30°-60°-90° triangles in a diagram of the given information. Since the height of the first tree is 36 m, the horizontal distance from the first to the second tree is $12\sqrt{3}$ m. Thus, the height of the second tree is 12 m more than the height of the first tree, so the height of the second tree, in m, is $\boxed{48}$.

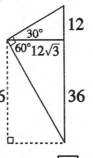

Problem 3-5

Method I: Look at the ship that leaves Miami on the 7th. At the dock, it meets the ship that left Montreal on the 1st (don't count it). Then, it meets all Miami-bound ships until, at the dock in Montreal, it meets the ship leaving on the 13th (don't count it either). The total number of ships it meets is $\boxed{11}$.

Method II: The ships approach each other at twice the speed each is making relative to the water. Therefore, the ship passes one ship going in the opposite direction every 12 hours. That's two each day, except don't count a ship that just arrives as another ship departs. On a 6-day trip, the total is 11.

Problem 3-6

Method I: The first ellipse has its major axis on the x-axis. The length of its major axis is 12 and the length of its minor axis is 8. The second ellipse has its major axis on the y-axis. Its major axis has length 18 and its minor axis has length 12. The ratio of the lengths of each set of axes is 2:3; so the ellipses are similar, with ratio of similitude $\dfrac{2}{3} = \boxed{2:3}$.

Method II: The larger (second) ellipse is obtained from the smaller (first) by the composition of a 90° rotation, centered at the origin, with a 150% dilation, also centered at the origin.

[**NOTE:** The ellipses $\dfrac{x^2}{4} + \dfrac{y^2}{9} = 1$ and $\dfrac{x^2}{36} + \dfrac{y^2}{16} = 1$ have ratio of similitude $\dfrac{1}{2}$ or 1:2.]

Contests written and compiled by Steven R. Conrad & Daniel Flegler   Mathematics Leagues Inc., © 1996

Problem 4-1

Method I: If $(x+1)(x-1) = 8$, then $x^2 = 9$. Finally, $(x^2+x)(x^2-x) = (9\pm3)(9\mp3) = 81-9 = \boxed{72}$.

Method II: If $(x+1)(x-1) = 8$, then $x^2 = 9$. Finally, $(x^2+x)(x^2-x) = x^2(x+1)(x-1) = 9\times8 = 72$.

Problem 4-2

The problem says that $7(x - 7) = 11(x - 11)$. The solution is $x = \boxed{18}$.

[**NOTE:** The solution to $a(x - a) = b(x - b)$ is $x = a + b$. In the given problem $a = 7$ and $b = 11$.]

Problem 4-3

When the hexagon is inscribed in the rectangle as shown, four $30°$-$60°$-$90°$ triangles (with the dimensions shown) are created in 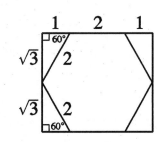 the corners of the rectangle. The rectangle has a width of 4, a height of $2\sqrt{3}$, and an area of $\boxed{8\sqrt{3}}$.

Problem 4-4

$\sec^2x = 1+\tan^2x = 1+\sin^2x+\cos^2x = 1+1 = \boxed{2}$.

Problem 4-5

$$a^2 - b^2 = (a - b)(a + b)$$
$$= (2\times 17^{3x^9-9x^{52}+1})(2\times 17^{9x^{52}-3x^9-1})$$
$$= 2\times 2\times 17^0$$
$$= \boxed{4}.$$

Problem 4-6

The two largest digits must be as far left as possible, so start one number with a 9 and the other with an 8. Where should you place the next two digits? Do you want 97 and 86, or 96 and 87? Use your calculator. You'll discover that *when the sum of two numbers is constant, their product increases as the numbers get closer.* Therefore, "attach" the smaller digit, 6, to the larger number, 9, to get 96; and "attach" the larger digit, 7, to the smaller number, 8, to get 87. The numbers will be as close as possible, and their product will then be as large as possible. Use this procedure again to get 964 and 875, and then once more to get 9642 and 8753. Finally, attach the "1" to 8753, the smaller of the two numbers obtained so far. At the end, the smaller number is 9642 and the larger number is $\boxed{87531}$.

Contests written and compiled by Steven R. Conrad & Daniel Flegler   Mathematics Leagues Inc., © 1997

Problem 5-1

Method I: The rectangle consists of 8 triangles, so the area of the rectangle is $8 \times 20 = \boxed{160}$.

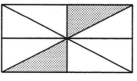

Method II: Since the length of each triangle is half the length ℓ of the rectangle, and the width of each triangle is half the width w of the rectangle, the area of each triangle is $\left(\frac{1}{2}\right)\left(\frac{\ell}{2}\right)\left(\frac{w}{2}\right)$. Therefore, $\frac{\ell w}{8} = 20$, and $\ell w = 160$.

Problem 5-2

The smallest such positive integer will have as few digits as possible, so all but the first digit must be 9's. Since $9 \times 221 = 1989$, we need 221 9's. Then, since $9 \times 221 + 8 = 1997$, the integer we seek is 899...99. This number has a total of $\boxed{222}$ digits.

Problem 5-3

Method I: $P(x+c) = (x+c)^3 + 6(x+c)^2 + 7(x+c) + 2$, a polynomial whose second-degree term is $3cx^2 + 6x^2$. This will equal 0 when $c = \boxed{-2}$.

Method II: The sum of all the roots = −(coefficient of the x^2 term) ÷ (lead coefficient) = −6. If we add 2 to each root, the sum of the roots will be 0; so $c = -2$.

Problem 5-4

If Brian were best, then Ali and Keith both told the truth. If Marina were best, then Ali and Brian both told the truth. If Keith were best, then everyone except Keith told the truth. Finally, if Ali were best, then only Brian told the truth. So $\boxed{\text{Ali}}$ is best.

Problem 5-5

Let the lengths of the legs be a and b, with $a > b$. We are told that $(a+b)^2 = 1000$ and that $(ab)^2 = 2500$. From this, we conclude that $a^2 + b^2 + 2ab = 1000$ and $2ab = 100$. Subtracting, $a^2 + b^2 = 900$. The length of the hypotenuse = $\sqrt{a^2 + b^2} = \boxed{30}$.

[**SINCE** $a+b = \sqrt{a^2 + 2ab + b^2} = \sqrt{1000}$ and $a-b = \sqrt{a^2 - 2ab + b^2} = \sqrt{800}$, such a triangle does exist.]

Problem 5-6

This is a very difficult problem. Here's one solution:

Since $(2\cos\theta - 1)(2\cos\theta + 1) = 4\cos^2\theta - 1 = 2(2\cos^2\theta) - 1 = 2(\cos 2\theta + 1) - 1 = 2\cos 2\theta + 1$, it follows that $2\cos\theta - 1 = \frac{2\cos 2\theta + 1}{2\cos\theta + 1}$ is an identity. In this identity, successively replace θ first by x, then by $2x$, then by $4x$, and finally by $8x$, to rewrite the original expression as

$$\frac{(2\cos 16x + 1)(2\cos 8x + 1)(2\cos 4x + 1)(2\cos 2x + 1)}{(2\cos 8x + 1)(2\cos 4x + 1)(2\cos 2x + 1)(2\cos x + 1)}.$$

Reduce the common factors to obtain $\frac{2\cos 16x + 1}{2\cos x + 1}$, a fraction which equals 1 if and only if $\cos 16x = \cos x$. But, $\cos 16x = \cos x$ only if $16x + x = 2k\pi$ or $16x - x = 2k\pi$. For the least positive solution, let $k = 1$. It follows that $x = \frac{2\pi}{17}$, so $(a,b) = \boxed{(2,17)}$.

[**NOTE:** Alternatively, transform $\cos 16x - \cos x = 0$ into $2\sin(17x/2)\sin(15x/2) = 0$. This equation is satisfied if and only if $17x/2 = k\pi$ or $15x/2 = k\pi$.]

Contests written and compiled by **Steven R. Conrad & Daniel Flegler**   Mathematics Leagues Inc., © 1997

Problem 6-1

Method I: Clearing fractions, $-6 + \sqrt{36 - 4c} = 8$. Rearranging terms and squaring, $36 - 4c = 196$. Solving, $c = \boxed{-40}$.

Method II: The given equation tells us that 4 is a root of the quadratic equation $x^2 + 6x + c = 0$. Substituting $x = 4$, we get $c = -40$.

Problem 6-2

When polynomial equations are multiplied, all factors of either original equation are factors of the product, and *vice versa*. In this problem, the solution set of the new equation is $\{0, 1, 2, 3, 4\}$, the union of the solution sets of the original equations. The number of solutions is $\boxed{5}$.

Problem 6-3

A side of A is 12 and a side of B is 10, so a side of the smallest square is $12 - 10 = 2$. A side of the square below the smallest is $10 - 2 = 8$. A side of the remaining square is $8 - 2 = 6$. The longer dimension of the shaded rectangle plus a side of the 6×6 square equals $12 + 2 = 14$. Therefore, the long side of the shaded rectangle is $14 - 6 = 8$, the shorter side is 6, and the area is $\boxed{48}$.

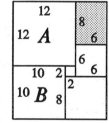

Problem 6-4

Convert to the exponential equation $2^{3-x} = 9 - 2^x$. This becomes $\frac{8}{2^x} = 9 - 2^x$. Now, let $y = 2^x$ and clear fractions to get $y^2 - 9y + 8 = 0$. Since $y = 1$ or $y = 8$, it follows that $2^x = 1$ or $2^x = 8$. In terms of x, the solutions are $\boxed{0, 3}$.

Problem 6-5

With a fair coin, $P(3\text{ heads}) = \frac{1}{8}$. With a two-headed coin, $P(3\text{ heads}) = 1$. Therefore, it's 8 times as likely that the coin landed heads up all three times because it was two-headed than because of tosses with a fair coin. Therefore, the probability that the coin was two-headed is $\boxed{\frac{8}{9}}$.

Problem 6-6

Method I: If we rewrite the original inequality as $\frac{3990}{3992} < \frac{a}{b} < \frac{3992}{3994}$, it appears reasonable to guess that the least such b is $\boxed{3993}$.

[**NOTE:** Method II gives a *proof* that 3993 is correct.]

Method II: First rewrite the original inequality as $1 - \frac{1}{1996} < \frac{a}{b} < 1 - \frac{1}{1997}$. Subtract 1 throughout to get $\frac{-1}{1996} < \frac{a}{b} - 1 < \frac{-1}{1997}$, or $\frac{1}{1997} < \frac{a'}{b} < \frac{1}{1996}$, where $a' = b - a$. Now, since $\frac{1}{1997} < \frac{a'}{b}$ implies that $b < 1997a'$, and $\frac{a'}{b} < \frac{1}{1996}$ implies that $1996a' < b$, we see that $1996a' < b < 1997a'$. The least positive integer b occurs when $a' = 2$ and $b = 3993$.

Contests written and compiled by Steven R. Conrad & Daniel Flegler   Mathematics Leagues Inc., © 1997

Problem 1-1

Method I: Let $\sqrt{n^3 + 1} = x$, where x is an integer. Square and subtract 1 from both sides to get $n^3 = x^2 - 1 = (x - 1)(x + 1)$. Since n^3 can be written as a product of two integers that differ by 2, n^3 can be $8 = (2)(4)$, $-1 = (-1)(1)$, $0 = (0)(2)$ or $(-2)(0)$. Finally, $n = \boxed{-1, 0, 2}$.

Method II: On a graphing calculator with a table feature, let $y_1 = \sqrt[3]{(x-1)(x+1)}$. Now check the table to see that if $x = -1$, 0, 1, and 3, then y_1 has one of the integral values -1, 0, 2.

Problem 1-2

There are 8 difficult algebra questions, so there are $60 - 8 = 52$ other algebra questions. Since there are 80 non-difficult questions, and 52 of these involve algebra, the number of questions that are neither difficult nor involve algebra is $80 - 52 = \boxed{28}$.

[The information is summarized in the Venn diagram.]

Problem 1-3

As seen at the right,

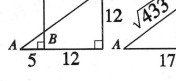

$AD = \boxed{\sqrt{433}}$.

Problem 1-4

Let $(3-b, 0)$ and $(0, b)$ be the x- and y-intercepts of a 3-line. The slope of any such line is $b/(b-3)$. Since the line passes through $(-2, -4)$, it follows that $(b+4)/2 = b/(b-3)$, so $b^2 - b - 12 = (b-4)(b+3) = 0$. One *3-line* goes through $(-1, 0)$ and $(0, 4)$; the other contains $(0, -3)$ and $(6, 0)$. The sum of the y-intercepts is $4 + (-3) = \boxed{1}$.

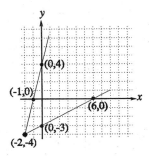

Problem 1-5

Method I: The polynomial $(x-1)$ has a coefficient sum of $1 - 1 = 0$. Next, $(x-1)(x-2) = x^2 - 3x + 2$ has a coefficient sum of $1 - 3 + 2 = 0$. The pattern continues: The sum is 0 whenever $(x-1)$ is a factor of the original polynomial. Here's why: If the polynomial were just $(x-1)$, the sum would be 0. Multiplying 0 by other factors causes no change, so the sum remains $\boxed{0}$.

Method II: When all binomials are multiplied, the result has the form $f(x) = ax^{1997} + bx^{1996} + \ldots$. If we let $x = 1$, then $f(1) = a + b + \ldots =$ the sum of the coefficients $= (1-1)(1-2) \times \ldots = 0$.

Problem 1-6

The only 10-digit decreasing number is 9876543210. For every selection of digits, there's just one way to arrange the digits in decreasing order. There are $\binom{10}{9}$ ways to choose 9 of the 10 digits, so there are $\binom{10}{9} = 10$ such 9-digit decreasing numbers. The number of decreasing numbers is $\binom{10}{10} + \binom{10}{9} + \ldots + \binom{10}{3} + \binom{10}{2}$. This is the sum of all but the last two entries in the 10th row of Pascal's Triangle. This sum is $\boxed{1013}$.

Contests written and compiled by Steven R. Conrad & Daniel Flegler   Mathematics Leagues Inc., © 1997

Problem 2-1

The last digit of the product is 5, so one reversible numbers ends with a 5, and the other begins with a 5. The last digit of the product is odd, so both reversible numbers are odd. Since $599 \times 995 = 596\,005$, the smallest number is less than 599. The first digit of the larger number must be a 9, since 599×900 is too small. The numbers are of the form $5?9 \times 9?5$, so use calculator trial and error to discover that $579 \times 975 = 564\,525$. Hence the numbers are $\boxed{579 \text{ and } 975}$.

Problem 2-2

A diagonal divides a square into two 45°-45°-90° right triangles. Thus, $\triangle FPD$ and $\triangle EPD$ are congruent isosceles right triangles, and $EP = PD = FP = 6$. Finally, $BD = BP + PD = 12 + 6 = \boxed{18}$.

Problem 2-3

The median is $(2^{k+1} + 2^{k+2}) \div 2 = 2^k + 2^{k+1}$. Divide by the smallest number, 2^k, to get $(2^k + 2^{k+1}) \div 2^k = 1 + 2^1 = \boxed{3}$.

Problem 2-4

Method I: There are seven missing digits between the first and second 9's shown. The sum of any four consecutive digits is 24, so the sum of any eight consecutive digits is $2 \times 24 = 48$. If the sum of the seven missing digits is S, then $S + 9 = 48$, so $S = \boxed{39}$.

Method II: The 16-digit sequence must be of the form *abcdabcdabcdabcd*, where $a = 7$, $c = 1$, $d = 9$, and $b = 24 - (7+1+9) = 7$. Hence, the sequence is 77**19**7719771**97**719, and the required sum is 39.

Problem 2-5

The sum of the roots of $ax^2 + bx + c = 0$ is $-b/a$, and the product of the roots is c/a. The root sum $= -2t-2 < 0$, so $t > -1$. Their product is $9t-5 > 0$, so $t > 5/9$. The roots are unequal, so the discriminant is $4(t+1)^2 - 4(9t-5) = 4(t-6)(t-1) > 0$; thus, $t < 1$ or $t > 6$. To satisfy all three conditions simultaneously, $5/9 < t < 1$ or $t > 6$. Hence, $t = \boxed{7}$.

Problem 2-6

The areas vary directly as the squares of the corresponding linear dimensions, and the volumes vary directly as the cubes of these same dimensions. If the areas are x^2, $(x+1)^2$, $(x+2)^2$, and $(x+3)^2$, then the volumes are kx^3, $k(x+1)^3$, $k(x+2)^3$, and $k(x+3)^3$. Thus, $k[x^3 + (x+1)^3 + (x+2)^3] = k(x+3)^3$. Dividing through by k, $x^3 + (x+1)^3 + (x+2)^3 = (x+3)^3$.

Method I: On a graphing calculator, set $y = x^3 + (x+1)^3 + (x+2)^3 - (x+3)^3$. The real root is 3, so $x = 3$. The area of the largest solid is $(x+3)^2 = \boxed{36}$.

Method II: Let $X = x-3$. Then, $(X+3)^3 + (X+4)^3 + (X+5)^3 = (X+6)^3$, so $2X(X^2+3X+21) = 0$. Since $X^2+3X+21 = 0$ has no real solutions, it follows that $2X = 0$. Since $X = x-3$, $x = 3$, and $(x+3)^2 = 36$.

Contests written and compiled by Steven R. Conrad & Daniel Flegler   Mathematics Leagues Inc., © 1997

Problem 3-1

The smallest possible integral difference between terms is 1. There are two more terms after 19, so the final three terms could be 19, 20, $\boxed{21}$.

Problem 3-2

In 60 minutes, Flash runs $20 - 15 = 5$ more laps than Speedy. The number of minutes it takes Flash to travel one more lap than Speedy is $60 \div 5 = \boxed{12}$.

Problem 3-3

The sum of the digits of a multiple of 9 is divisible by 9. We want the smallest positive integer that has only even digits and whose digits have a sum of 18. In the smallest such integer, the leftmost digit is a 2 and the other digits are 8's. The number is $\boxed{288}$.

Problem 3-4

Method I: If $y = x^3$, then $\left(\sqrt[3]{y}\right)^y = 3$. Cubing, $y^y = 3^3$ and $y = 3$. Since $y = x^3$, $x^3 = 3$ and $x = \boxed{\sqrt[3]{3}}$.

Method II: On a graphing calculator, $y = x^{\left(x^3\right)} - 3$ crosses the x–axis at $x = 1.44224957030\ldots.$

[**NOTE:** Some calculators calculate x^{x^3} from left to right, instead of the mathematically correct way, right to left. They do this when you forget to use parentheses. If you got $1.3198\ldots$ as an answer, please try again. This time, if you use the parentheses indicated in the question, you'll get the right answer, 1.442.]

Problem 3-5

Let $\langle x \rangle$ represent the *fractional part* of x. Consequently, $0 \le \langle x \rangle < 1$. Then $x = [x] + \langle x \rangle$, so $x - [x] = \langle x \rangle$. Let $S = [1a + 9b + 9c + 8d] - 1[a] - 9[b] - 9[c] - 8[d] = [1a - 1[a] + 9b - 9[b] + 9c - 9[c] + 8d - 8[d]] = [1\langle a \rangle + 9\langle b \rangle + 9\langle c \rangle + 8\langle d \rangle]$. If $\langle a \rangle, \langle b \rangle, \langle c \rangle, \langle d \rangle = 0$, then $S = 0$. Since $\langle a \rangle, \langle b \rangle, \langle c \rangle, \langle d \rangle < 1$, we have $S < 1 + 9 + 9 + 8 = 27$. Hence, $0 \le S \le 26$, and there are $\boxed{27}$ different possible integer values of S.

Problem 3-6

Method I: Since $\triangle AYD$ and $\triangle YDC$ share the same altitude from D, the ratio of their areas equals the ratio of their bases, 5:4. Likewise for $\triangle BDX$ and $\triangle XDC$. If we let the area of $\triangle AYD = 5x =$ the area of $\triangle BDX$, then the area of $\triangle YDC = 4x =$ the area of $\triangle XDC$. Since the area of $\triangle CAX$ is 18, we have $18 = 5x + 4x + 4x = 13x$. Solving, $x = \frac{18}{13}$, and $5x = \frac{90}{13}$. Since the area of $\triangle ABX$ is $\frac{1}{2}(5)(9) = \frac{45}{2}$, the area of $\triangle ABD$ is $\frac{45}{2} - \frac{90}{13} = \boxed{\frac{405}{26}}$.

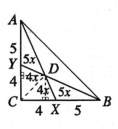

Method II: The equation of line BY is $y = -\frac{4}{9}x + 4$, while that of AX is $y = -\frac{9}{4}x + 9$. These intersect at $\left(\frac{36}{13}, \frac{36}{13}\right)$, so $A(\triangle ABD) = A(\triangle ABC) - [A(\triangle ACX) + A(\triangle BDX)] = \frac{1}{2}(9)(9) - [\frac{1}{2}(9)(4) + \frac{1}{2}\left(\frac{36}{13}\right)(5)] = \frac{81}{2} - \frac{324}{13} = \frac{405}{26}$.

Contests written and compiled by Steven R. Conrad & Daniel Flegler   Mathematics Leagues Inc., © 1998

Problem 4-1

If you were born in the 20th century, then the sum of the last two digits of the year in which you were born, plus your age on your birthday in 1998, would be equal to 98. The two given statements are equivalent to $ab + cd = 98$ and $cd + ab = 98$. Since any pair of whole numbers whose sum is 98 is correct, we see that a correct answer is any one ordered pair of the form (x,y), with x,y whole numbers for which $x+y = 98$.

Problem 4-2

Dividing, $\sqrt{\frac{3/8}{6}} = \sqrt{\frac{1}{16}} = \frac{1}{4} = 25\%$, so $p = \boxed{25}$.

[**NOTE:** The value of p is 25, *not* 25%. Reread the question to understand why "25%" is *not* a correct answer.]

Problem 4-3

Method I: The rectangles are similar, so the diagonals of the two rectangles overlap with a common endpoint. The diagonals have lengths 10 and 15, so the distance between their centers is $\frac{1}{2}(15-10) = \boxed{2\frac{1}{2}}$.

Method II: Let the common vertex be at $(0,0)$. The smaller rectangle's opposite vertex is $(8,6)$, the larger rectangle's opposite vertex is $(12,9)$. The centers are at $(4,3)$ and $(6,4.5)$. Now use the distance formula.

Problem 4-4

Method I: Since $(1+i)^2 = 2i$ and $(1-i)^2 = -2i$, we can square both sides of both equations one more time to get $(1+i)^4 = (2i)^2 = -4$ and also $(1-i)^4 = (-2i)^2 = -4$. Therefore, the least such n is $\boxed{4}$.

Method II: Note that $1+i = \sqrt{2}\,\text{cis}\,45°$ and $1-i = \sqrt{2}\,\text{cis}\,(-45°)$. By DeMoivre's Theorem, the 4th power of each will coincide.

Problem 4-5

The equation of line OP is $y = -\sqrt{3}\,x$; so points on this line satisfy $y^2 = 3x^2$, or $x^2 = y^2/3$. Substituting this into the equation of the ellipse, $\frac{y^2}{12} + \frac{y^2}{9} = 1$, or $7y^2 = 36$. Since $y < 0$, the coordinates of P are $\boxed{\left(\frac{2\sqrt{3}}{\sqrt{7}}, \frac{-6}{\sqrt{7}}\right)}$.

Problem 4-6

In a 2-term sum, the average term would be 50 (an impossibility). Similarly, there can be no such 3-term sum and no such 4-term sum. The 5-term sum (average term 20) is $18+19+20+21+22$. The only other such sequence is $9+10+11+12+13+14+15+16$. The average of its 8 terms is $12\frac{1}{2}$. Since no other such sums are possible, the answer is $18 \times 9 = \boxed{162}$.

Problem 5-1

Since $26x = 27x^2$, it follows that $x(27x-26) = 0$. The values of x for which this is true are $\boxed{0, \frac{26}{27}}$.

Problem 5-2

Since $143\,000\,000 = 143 \times 10^6 = 11 \times 13 \times 2^6 \times 5^6$, its largest prime factor is $\boxed{13}$.

Problem 5-3

Method I: The probability that either strikes it rich (henceforth, wins) is $\frac{1}{8}$, so the probability that either does not strike it rich (loses) is $\frac{7}{8}$. Since $P(\text{Al wins, Barb loses}) = P(\text{Barb wins, Al loses}) = \frac{1}{8} \times \frac{7}{8} = \frac{7}{64}$, and $P(\text{both win}) = \frac{1}{8} \times \frac{1}{8} = \frac{1}{64}$, the probability that at least one of them wins is $\frac{7}{64} + \frac{7}{64} + \frac{1}{64} = \boxed{\frac{15}{64}}$.

Method II: Let A mean that Al wins, and B mean Barb wins. $P(A \cup B) = P(A) + P(B) - P(A \cap B)$, it follows that $P(A \cup B) = \frac{1}{8} + \frac{1}{8} - \frac{1}{64} = \frac{15}{64}$.

Method III: With A and B as defined in Method II, $P(A) = P(B) = \frac{1}{8}$, so $P(A') = P(B') = \frac{7}{8}$. Since $P(A' \cap B') = P(A')P(B') = \frac{7}{8} \times \frac{7}{8} = \frac{49}{64}$, it follows that $P(A \cup B) = 1 - \frac{49}{64} = \frac{15}{64}$.

Problem 5-4

Method I: $\frac{1}{3}(\log_{12}3 + \log_{12}6 + \log_{12}8) = \frac{1}{3}(\log_{12}144) = \frac{1}{3}(2) = \boxed{\frac{2}{3}}$.

Method II: Use the change of base theorem. Since $\log_b a = \frac{\log a}{\log b}$, the answer $= \frac{1}{3}\left(\frac{\log 3}{\log 12} + \frac{\log 6}{\log 12} + \frac{\log 8}{\log 12}\right)$
$= \frac{1}{3}\left(\frac{\log 3 + \log 6 + \log 8}{\log 12}\right) = \frac{1}{3}\left(\frac{\log 144}{\log 12}\right) = \frac{1}{3}\left(\frac{2\log 12}{\log 12}\right) = \frac{2}{3}$.

[**NOTE:** To use a calculator, compute the value of the second line of Method II. The result is $\frac{2}{3} = 0.\overline{6}$.]

Problem 5-5

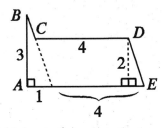

Extend $\overline{BC}$ until it reaches $\overline{AE}$. This creates a rt $\triangle$ with $\overline{BA}$ as a leg and a $\square$ with $\overline{CD}$ as a side. The $\square$'s area is $4 \times 2 = 8$. Since $\overline{AE} = 5$, the base of the $\triangle$ is $5-4 = 1$. The rt $\triangle$ has an area of $(3 \times 1)/2 = 1.5$. Finally, the total area of the pentagon is $8 + 1.5 = \boxed{9.5}$.

Problem 5-6

Method I: P isn't linear. It can't be quadratic: we'd have a $\sqrt{6}$ term. Since $(\sqrt{3} + \sqrt{2})^3 = 9\sqrt{3} + 11\sqrt{2}$, if P is cubic, it has no quadratic term and no constant. If $P(x) = ax^3 + cx$, then $a(\sqrt{3} + \sqrt{2})^3 + c(\sqrt{3} + \sqrt{2}) = a(9\sqrt{3} + 11\sqrt{2}) + c(\sqrt{3} + \sqrt{2}) = (9a+c)\sqrt{3} + (11a+c)\sqrt{2} = \sqrt{3} - \sqrt{2}$. Hence $9a+c = 1$ and $11a+c = -1$, so $a = -1, c = 10$, and $P(x) = \boxed{-x^3 + 10x}$.

[We call this *The Method of Undetermined Coefficients.*]

Method II: Let $x = \sqrt{3} + \sqrt{2}$. Square both sides to get $x^2 = 3 + 2\sqrt{6} + 2 = 5 + 2\sqrt{6}$; so $x^2 - 5 = 2\sqrt{6}$. Squaring again, $x^4 - 10x^2 + 1 = 0$. Since $x = \sqrt{3} + \sqrt{2}$, and since $\sqrt{3} + \sqrt{2}$ and $\sqrt{3} - \sqrt{2}$ are reciprocals, it follows that $\frac{1}{x} = \frac{1}{\sqrt{3} + \sqrt{2}} = \sqrt{3} - \sqrt{2}$. From before, we know that $-x^4 + 10x^2 = 1$. Divide by x to get $-x^3 + 10x = \frac{1}{x} = \sqrt{3} - \sqrt{2}$; hence $P(x) = -x^3 + 10x$.

[**NOTE:** $\frac{1}{x}$ is *not* a polynomial, so $P(x) \neq \frac{1}{x}$.]

Contests written and compiled by Steven R. Conrad & Daniel Flegler   Mathematics Leagues Inc., © 1998

Problem 6-1

Since 17 is prime, any positive integral root comes from $(x-17)(x-1) = x^2 - 18x + 17 = 0$, so $a = \boxed{-18}$.

Problem 6-2

The minimum value of $|\pm 1998 \pm 1999 \pm 2000|$ is $|1998 + 1999 - 2000| = |2000 - 1998 - 1999| = \boxed{1997}$.

Problem 6-3

Since $1^2 + 1^2 + 1^2 + 1^2 = 2^2$, the least possible perimeter is $1 + 1 + 1 + 1 + 2 = \boxed{6}$.

Problem 6-4

Since $f(x) = f(x+6) = f(x+6+6) = f(x+2+10) = f(x+2)$, we know that $f(x) = f(x+2)$ for all real x. Hence, $f(22) = f(24) = f(26) = \ldots = f(44)$, so $f(44) = f(22) = \boxed{22}$.

Problem 6-5

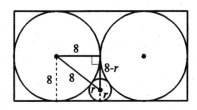

In the right triangle shown, the hypotenuse is $8+r$ and the legs are 8 and $8-r$. By the Pythagorean Thm., $8^2 + (8-r)^2 = (8+r)^2$; so $r = 2$, and the area of the small circle is $\boxed{4\pi}$.

Problem 6-6

Since $A + B + C = 180°$, $A + C = 180° - B$, and $\tan(A + C) = \tan(180° - B) = -\tan B$. Expanding, $\frac{\tan A + \tan C}{1 - \tan A \tan C} = -\tan B$. The tangents are in arithmetic sequence, so $\tan C - \tan B = \tan B - \tan A$; so $\tan B = \frac{\tan A + \tan C}{2}$. Since $\tan A + \tan C \neq 0$, $\frac{-(\tan A + \tan C)}{1 - \tan A \tan C} = \frac{\tan A + \tan C}{2}$. Clearing fractions and simplifying, $\tan A \tan C = \boxed{3}$.

Problem 1-1

If 3 of the talks are 1 hour each, then the 4th talk will be as long as possible, 2 hours or $\boxed{120}$ minutes.

[**NOTE:** The answer *2 hours* is incorrect because the wording of the question requires that the answer be given in minutes.]

Problem 1-2

Since $6666 \times 33 = 219978$, we have shown that the product can contain the digits 1, 2, 7, 8, and 9. Thus, the digits that don't appear are $\boxed{0, 3, 4, 5, 6}$.

[**NOTE:** If n is the number of 3's used at the start, it can be proven that all such products have the form $22\ldots22199\ldots\ldots9977\ldots778$, where $(n-1)$ 2's are followed by a single 1, then n 9's, then $(n-1)$ 7's, then a final 8, for a total of $3n$ digits.]

Problem 1-3

Since the y-intercept is 6, the altitude to $\overline{AC}$ has a length of 6. The x-intercepts are at k and -4. Since $k>0$, $AC = 4+k$. The area of $\triangle ABC = 6(4+k)/2 = 12 + 3k = 21$. Solving, $k = \boxed{3}$.

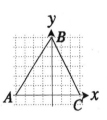

Problem 1-4

Method I: We are given $m+h = 23$ and $m^2+h^2 = 17^2$. Since $h = 23-m$, $m^2+(23-m)^2 = 17^2$. Since the minute hand's length exceeds that of the hour hand, $m = 15$, $h = 23-15 = 8$, and $m-h = 15-8 = \boxed{7}$.

Method II: We are given $m+h = 23$ and $m^2+h^2 = 17^2$. Squaring the first equation and subtracting the second, we have $2mh = 240$. Next, $m^2+h^2-2mh = 289-240 = 49 = (m-h)^2$, so $m-h = 7$.

Problem 1-5

Since a, b, c are roots, we have $a^3+78a+666 = 0$, $b^3+78b+666 = 0$, and $c^3+78c+666 = 0$. Adding these 3 equations, $a^3+b^3+c^3+78(a+b+c)+1998 = 0$. The coefficient of x^2 is 0, so the sum of the roots of $x^3+78x+666 = 0$ is 0. Thus, $a^3+b^3+c^3+78(0)+1998 = 0$, and $a^3+b^3+c^3 = \boxed{-1998}$.

Problem 1-6

The 13th day of a month will fall on a Friday if and only if the 1st day of that month falls on a Sunday. Separate the months by the rule that months A and B fall into the same group if and only if the 1st day of month A is on the same day of the week as the 1st day of month B. For a nonleap year, there are 7 groupings: {Jan, Oct}, {Feb, Mar, Nov}, {Apr, Jul}, {May}, {Jun}, {Aug}, and {Sep, Dec}. For a leap year, there are 7 different groupings: {Jan, Apr, Jul}, {Feb, Aug}, {Mar, Nov}, {May}, {Jun}, {Sep, Dec}, and {Oct}. For both leap years and nonleap years, the groups contain at most 3 months and at least 1 month. Hence, for any calendar year, the minimum number of Friday the 13th's is 1, the maximum is 3, and $(m,M) = \boxed{(1,3)}$.

The information above can be summarized in the chart that appears below.

When Jan 1st Falls on a	Nonleap Year	Leap Year
	Friday the 13th Will Occur in	
Monday	April, July	Sept., Dec.
Tuesday	Sept., Dec.	June
Wednesday	June	March, Nov.
Thursday	Feb., March, Nov.	Feb., Aug.
Friday	August	May
Saturday	May	October
Sunday	Jan., Oct.	Jan., April, July

Problem 2-1

Since T is not equilateral, T can't have sides 1, 1, 1. Also, T can't have sides 1, 1, 2, since the sum of the lengths of the two smaller sides of any triangle must exceed the length of the third side. Since T with sides 1, 2, 2 *is* a non-equilateral triangle, the minimum perimeter of triangle T is $1+2+2 = \boxed{5}$.

Problem 2-2

Write 74 and 54 as products with 2 common factors and 1 different: $74 = 1\times2\times37$ and $54 = 1\times2\times27$. The 4 numbers are 1, 2, 27, 37. Their product is $\boxed{1998}$.

Problem 2-3

Method I: Since $x \neq 0$, $x^5-x^4-x^3 = (x^3)(x^2-x-1) = 0$ implies that $x^2-x-1 = 0$. By the quadratic formula, the positive root is $x = \boxed{\dfrac{1 + \sqrt{5}}{2}}$.

Method II: Use a graphing calculator to sketch $y = x^5-x^4-x^3$. The positive root is $x = 1.618 \ldots$.

Problem 2-4

Since $ABCD$ is a square whose diagonals are each 12, $AB = 6\sqrt{2}$. This distance represents $2r$, so $r = 3\sqrt{2}$ and the area of one circle is $\pi(3\sqrt{2})^2 = \boxed{18\pi}$.

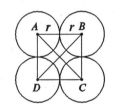

Problem 2-5

Since the radicand must be nonnegative, $x^2-3x+2 = (x-2)(x-1) \geq 0$. Solving, $x \geq 2$ or $x \leq 1$. Square both sides of the original inequality to get $x^2-3x+2 < x^2+6x+9$, or $x > -7/9$. The solutions, which are those values of x that satisfy the condition in the 3rd sentence *subject to* the conditions in the 2nd sentence, are $\boxed{\{x \mid -\frac{7}{9} < x \leq 1\} \cup \{x \mid x \geq 2\}}$.

[**NOTE:** The answer "$-7/9 < x \leq 1$ *or* $x \geq 2$" is also acceptable; we do not require set notation. However, **BOTH** conditions are required for credit. Answers giving only one condition do *not* receive credit.]

Problem 2-6

Method I: Extend $\overline{NM}$ till it meets the x-axis at $B(-2,0)$. M is the midpoint of $\overline{BN}$, so if A is on the x-axis, $\triangle ABN$ has twice the area of $\triangle AMN$.

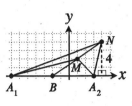

We seek all points A on the x-axis for which $\triangle ABN$ has area 10. The altitude from N to the x-axis is 4, so AB must be 5. A must be on the x-axis, 5 units from $B(-2,0)$. The possibilities are $\boxed{(-7,0),\ (3,0)}$.

Method II: When the x-coordinate of A is -1, 0, 1, the area is 1, 2, 3 respectively (computed by surrounding the triangle with a rectangle). This pattern continues to the left and to the right of $x = -2$.

Method III: By determinants, area $= \frac{1}{2}\begin{vmatrix} 1 & 2 & 1 \\ 4 & 4 & 1 \\ x & 0 & 1 \end{vmatrix} = \pm5$. The respective solutions for x are -7 and 3.

Method IV: There are four cases. Begin each by surrounding the triangle with a rectangle. The sum of the areas of the "excess" right $\triangle$s + the "excess" rectangle (if one appears) + 5 = the area of the surrounding rectangle, so solve for x.

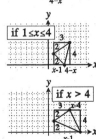

If $x \leq -2$, then $2(4 - x) + 3 + 6 + (1 - x) + 5 = 4(4 - x)$. Solving, $x = -7$.

If $-2 < x < 1$, then $(1-x) + 2(1-x) + 3 + 2(4-x) + 5 = 4(4-x)$. Solving, $x = 3$ (reject).

If $1 \leq x \leq 4$, then $(x-1) + 3 + (8-2x) + 5 = 12$. Solving, $x = 3$.

If $x > 4$, then $(x-1) + 3 + (2x-8) + 5 = 4(x-1)$. Solving, $x = 3$ (reject).

The third vertex could be located at $(-7,0)$ or $(3,0)$.

Contests written and compiled by Steven R. Conrad & Daniel Flegler   Mathematics Leagues Inc., © 1998

Problem 3-1

The lengths of the sides of the three squares are 3, 4, and 5. Since $\overline{AB}$ is the hypotenuse of a right triangle with legs 5 and 12, its length is $\boxed{13}$.

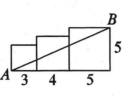

Problem 3-2

The given equation is equivalent to $a^2 + b^2 = c^2$. It's from the Pythagorean Theorem! The triple with the smallest sum is 3-4-5, so the answer is $\boxed{12}$.

Problem 3-3

Draw a perpendicular from the center of the circle to the chord, forming a 30°–60°–90° triangle with a 30° angle at P and with a hypotenuse of length 2. The distance sought is the length of the perpendicular, $\boxed{1}$.

Problem 3-4

Rewrite each term using base 3 and you'll get $3^{1998} + 3^{1998} + 3^{3n} = 3^{1999}$, or $3^{3n} = 3^{1999} - 3^{1998} - 3^{1998}$. Factoring, $3^{3n} = 3^{1998}(3 - 1 - 1)$. Therefore, $3^{3n} = 3^{1998}$; so $3n = 1998$ and $n = \boxed{666}$.

Problem 3-5

Guessing is the quickest way to do this problem. Here is a more mathematical approach: By long division, $\frac{x}{x-2} = 1 + \frac{2}{x-2}$ is integral if and only if $x-2$ is a factor of 2. This occurs when $x-2 = \pm 1$ or ± 2; that is, when $x = 0, 1, 3,$ or 4. In the same way, $\frac{x}{x-4}$ is integral if and only if $x-4$ is a factor of 4. This occurs when $x-4 = \pm 1, \pm 2,$ or ± 4; that is, when $x = 0, 2, 3, 5, 6,$ or 8. If $x = 0$ or 3, *both* fractions are integral. Both also make $\frac{x}{x-6}$ integral; so all three fractions will be integral for $x = \boxed{0, 3}$.

Problem 3-6

Method I: Consider the river to be a long train, with Pat walking from the front to the back of the train. Pat drops the hat, continues walking towards the back of the train for another 10 minutes, then turns around and walks back to where Pat dropped the hat. This takes another 10 minutes. Pat's total trip takes 20 minutes, and the hat (or the train) has moved 1 km in this time. Thus, the river moves 1 km in 20 min. In km/hr, its speed is $\boxed{\text{3 or 3 km/hr}}$.

Method II: Let c be the rate of the current and b be the rate of the boat in still water, both in km/hr. Let t be the number of hours it takes Pat to catch up to the hat after turning around. The hat traveled 1 km and was in the water for $(t+1/6)$ hrs; $c(t+1/6) = 1$. Hence $t = 1/c - 1/6$. The boat travels downstream for t hours at a rate of $(b+c)$ km/hr, so it travels a distance of $(b+c)t$ km downstream. It traveled upstream a distance of $(b-c)(1/6)$ km. It traveled 1 km more downstream than upstream, so $(b+c)t = (b-c)(1/6) + 1$. Substituting $t = 1/c - 1/6$ and simplifying, $c = 3$.

Contests written and compiled by Steven R. Conrad & Daniel Flegler   Mathematics Leagues Inc., © 1999

Problem 4-1

$\sqrt{45} = 3\sqrt{5} = \sqrt{5} + 2\sqrt{5} = \sqrt{5} + \sqrt{20}$, so $x = \boxed{20}$.

Problem 4-2

On Monday, he spent $0.30D$. When he spent 60% of the remainder, he spent $(0.60)(0.70D) = 0.42D$. This left him with $D - (0.30D + 0.42D) = 0.28D$. Since this was \$1 less than the amount he spent on Monday, $0.28D = 0.30D - 1$, so $0.02D = 1$ and $D = \boxed{50}$.

Problem 4-3

Factoring, $\dfrac{19^{98} + (342)(19^{97})}{19^{99}} = \dfrac{19^{97}(19 + 342)}{19^{99}} = \dfrac{19^{97}(361)}{19^{99}} = \dfrac{19^{97}(19^{2})}{19^{99}} = \dfrac{19^{99}}{19^{99}} = \boxed{1}$.

Problem 4-4

When we join the centers of the four circles whose radii are each 1, we form a square of side 2 and diagonal $2\sqrt{2}$. Let the length of a radius of the fifth circle be r. Then $2\sqrt{2} = 2r + 2$. Solving, $r = \boxed{\sqrt{2} - 1}$.

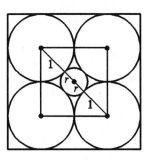

Problem 4-5

Method I: If two numbers have a fixed sum, their product is maximized when each number is half that sum. Since $x^2 + y^2 = 1$, when $x^2 = \frac{1}{2} = y^2$, the product $a = x^2 y^2$ has its maximum value, $\boxed{\frac{1}{4}}$.

Method II: Since $x^2 + y^2 = 1$, $y^2 = 1 - x^2$. Thus, $x^2 y^2 = a \Leftrightarrow x^2(1 - x^2) = a \Leftrightarrow x^2 - x^4 = a \Leftrightarrow x^4 - x^2 = -a$. Completing the square, we get $x^4 - x^2 + \frac{1}{4} = \frac{1}{4} - a$, or $\frac{1}{4} - (x^2 - \frac{1}{2})^2 = a$. If x^2 has the value $\frac{1}{2}$, then a can be as large as $\frac{1}{4}$. Otherwise, it is smaller; so $a \leq \frac{1}{4}$.

Method III: Both x and y are real, so x^2 and y^2 are both ≥ 0. Hence, $x^2 + y^2 = 1$ implies that $0 \leq x^2 \leq 1$. If we let $r = x^2$, then $0 \leq r \leq 1$. Since $x^2(1 - x^2) = a$ (for a proof, please see Method II), $r(1 - r) = a$. By the quadratic formula, $r = \frac{1 \pm \sqrt{1 - 4a}}{2}$. Substitute this into $0 \leq r \leq 1$, then multiply through by 2 to see that $0 \leq 1 \pm \sqrt{1 - 4a} \leq 2$. From this, $0 \leq 1 - 4a \leq 1$; and then $0 \leq a \leq \frac{1}{4}$.

Problem 4-6

If the hound's leap is $4x$, the fox's is $3x$, and the fox's 90 hound-leap headstart is a $360x$ headstart. While the hound took 4 leaps ($16x$), the fox took 5 ($15x$). The hound gained $1x$ every 4 leaps, so the hound needed $360 \times 4 = \boxed{1440}$ leaps to overcome the fox.

Contests written and compiled by Steven R. Conrad & Daniel Flegler   Mathematics Leagues Inc., © 1999

Problem 5-1

If $c > 2$, then $(1, c-1)$ and $(c-1, 1)$ are both solutions. Hence, the only such pair is $(1,1)$, and $c = \boxed{2}$.

Problem 5-2

Method I: The volume of a sphere is proportional to the cube of its diameter. If we divide through by the constant of proportionality, we get $d^3 = 3^3 + 4^3 + 5^3 = 216$, so $d = \boxed{6}$.

Method II: Let $2a$, $2b$, $2c$ be the diameters of the small balls. Their total volume is $\frac{4}{3}\pi(a^3+b^3+c^3) = \frac{4}{3}\pi(1.5^3+2^3+2.5^3) = \frac{4}{3}\pi(27) = \frac{4}{3}\pi(3^3)$. Since 3^3 is the cube of a radius of the final ball, its diameter is $2(3) = 6$.

Problem 5-3

Students numbered 20 through 98, 79 in all, are between student 19 and student 99. Similarly, there are 79 students between student 99 and student 19. Counting students 19 and 99 also, the total number of students is $79 + 79 + 1 + 1 = \boxed{160}$.

[**NOTE:** If you go back 18 students, you'll note that student 1 $(19-18)$ is opposite student 81 $(99-18)$. This makes the counting much easier.]

Problem 5-4

Since $x > 0$, we can multiply through by x without changing the direction of the inequality. Do this and combine terms to get $x^2 - 4x + 3 = (x-3)(x-1) \le 0$. Use the number line below to see that the inequality

is satisfied when $1 \le x \le 3$, an interval of length 2, but for no other positive numbers less than 10. The probability is $\boxed{\frac{2}{10}}$ or 0.2 or 1/5 or 20% or 2:10 or 1:5.

Problem 5-5

Since $n \approx 6.03 \times 10^{23}$, $\log_{10} n$ is between 23 and 24, and $[\log_{10} n] = 23$. Next, divide $n \approx 6.03 \times 10^{23}$ by 10^{23}. Finally, $[6.03] = \boxed{6}$.

Problem 5-6

Let f be the fractional part of the circle that is shaded, so $49 = \pi r^2 f$. Note that f also equals that fractional part of the circumference that bounds the shaded region, so $s = 2\pi r f$. Dividing these equations, we get $s/49 = 2/r$, or $rs = 98$. Since $28 = s+2r = s+2\left(\frac{98}{s}\right)$, $0 = s^2 - 28s + 196 = (s-14)^2$. Solving, $s = \boxed{14}$.

Contests written and compiled by Steven R. Conrad & Daniel Flegler   Mathematics Leagues Inc., © 1999

Problem 6-1

There is no carrying from the hundreds' column, so the missing digit in 1*64 is a 0, and the hundreds' digit of 1**9 must be a 9. There is carrying from the units' to the tens' column, but there is no carrying from the tens' to the hundreds' column; so the missing digit in the tens' column of 1*9 is a 0. Finally, the missing digit in the units' column of 82* is a 6, and the four-digit sum is $\boxed{1999}$.

82*	826
1*9	109
1*64	1064
1**9	1999

Problem 6-2

This is equivalent to asking for two times the least possible area of a right triangle whose sides all have integral length. The smallest such right triangle has sides 3, 4, and 5. The smallest such rectangle has dimensions 3 and 4, and its diagonals are both 5. Its area is $\boxed{12}$.

Problem 6-3

Use right triangle trigonometry in the diagram at the right, where the angles have degree-measures as indicated. The length of each side of the large pentagon is $2\cos 24°$, so $x = \boxed{24 \text{ or } 24°}$.

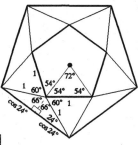

Problem 6-4

The roots of $ax^2+bx+c = 0$ have a sum of $-b/a$ and a product of c/a. The roots of $x^2-3x-3 = 0$ have a sum of $3 = r+s$ and a product of $-3 = rs$. Finally, $(r+s)-3(rs) = 3-3(-3) = \boxed{12}$.

Problem 6-5

It is easy to guess $f(1) = 1$, but the proof is involved. From the given, $f^{-1}(f(1)) = \frac{1}{f(f(1))}$. From the definition of an inverse, $f^{-1}(f(1)) = 1$. Hence $1 = \frac{1}{f(f(1))}$, or $f(f(1)) = 1$. Apply the inverse to both sides to get $f(1) = f^{-1}(1)$. The given implies that $f^{-1}(1) = \frac{1}{f(1)}$, so $f(1) = \frac{1}{f(1)}$. Next, $(f(1))^2 = 1$. Since $f(1) > 0$, it follows that $f(1) = \boxed{1}$.

[**NOTE:** Such functions are discussed in the September, 1981 issue of *Mathematics Magazine*, pp. 185-89.]

Problem 6-6

If the fixed constant is r, then the 7th term $\geq 200r^6$. If $r \geq 2$, then the 7th term $\geq 200(2^6) = 12800$. Since that's too large, but the terms do increase, $1 < r < 2$. Let $r = m/n$, with m and n integers with no common integral factor greater than 1. To make all terms integral, the first term must be divisible by n as many times as we multiply by r. To get 7 terms, the first term must be divisible by n^6. If $n = 3$, the first term is divisible by $3^6 = 729$, and the least r is 4/3. The sequence starts 729, 972, 1296, 1728, 2304. The next term exceeds 3000. To make n smaller, let $n = 2$; so the first term is divisible by $2^6 = 64$. The least multiple of 64 bigger than 200 is $4\times64 = 256$. With $n = 2$, the least r is 3/2. The resulting sequence is 256, 384, 576, 864, 1296, 1944, 2916; its largest term is $\boxed{2916}$.

Contests written and compiled by Steven R. Conrad & Daniel Flegler   **Mathematics Leagues Inc., © 1999**

Problem 1-1

If $x = 10t + u$, then $y = 10u + t$; hence, $x - y = 9(t - u)$, which is a multiple of 9. Since $x \neq y$, the least possible value of $|x - y|$, which occurs when t and u differ by 1, is $\boxed{9}$.

Problem 1-2

By the Pythagorean Theorem, the area of the square on the hypotenuse = the sum of the areas of the squares on the other two sides = $19 + 99 = \boxed{118}$.

Problem 1-3

Since 1 is *not* a prime, the set of primes below 50 is {2, 3, 5, 7, 11, 13, 17, 19, 23, 29, 31, 37, 41, 43, 47}. Start the counting by listing every product that has the form $2 \times$ (a different prime less than 50). You get:

$2 \times (3, 5, 7, 11, 13, \dots, 41, 43, 47)$	14 products
$3 \times (5, 7, 11, 13, 17, 19, 23, 29, 31)$	9 products
$5 \times (7, 11, 13, 17, 19)$	5 products
$7 \times (11, 13)$	2 products

The number of integers < 100 expressible as a product of two different primes is $14+9+5+2 = \boxed{30}$.

Problem 1-4

Method I: Since $\frac{1}{640} = 0.0015625$, the least value of x is $\boxed{15625}$.

Method II: Factor 640, then introduce any factors needed to turn the denominator into a power of 10:
$$\frac{1}{640} = \frac{1}{2^6 \times 5 \times 2} = \frac{1}{2^7 \times 5} = \frac{5^6}{2^7 \times 5^7} = \frac{5^6}{10^7} = \frac{15625}{10^7}.$$

Problem 1-5

The average age of the b boys was g, so the total of all their ages was bg. The average age of the g girls was b, so the total of all their ages was bg. The total of the ages of all the students was $2bg$. Together with their teacher, the total of all their ages was $2bg+42$, and the total number of people was $b+g+1$. Rewrite the equation $\frac{2bg+42}{b+g+1} = b+g$ as $b^2+g^2+b+g = 42$. By trial and error, the only positive integer solutions are $(b,g) = (5,3)$ or $(3,5)$. In either case, $b+g = \boxed{8}$.

Problem 1-6

Let S be the sum of the numbers in each shaded four-triangle. The sums are equal, so $S = a+b+c+d$, $S = b+e+f+g$, and $S = d+g+h+i$. Adding, $3S = (a+b+c+d+e+f+g+h+i) + (b+d+g)$. The sum of all the integers from 1 to 9 is 45, so $3S = 45+(b+d+g)$. Dividing by 3, $S = 15 + (b+d+g)/3$. To make S have the least possible integral value, we must make $(b+d+g)$ divisible by 3 and as small as possible. The least multiple of 3 obtainable by adding 3 different one-digit positive integers is $1+2+3 = 6$, so the least possible value of S is $15+(6/3) = 15+2 = \boxed{17}$.

[**NOTE:** One arrangement in which each four-triangle has a sum of 17 is shown at the right. Several variations of this arrangement also have a sum of 17.]

Contests written and compiled by Steven R. Conrad & Daniel Flegler   © 1999 by Mathematics Leagues Inc.

Problem 2-1

Since $b > a > 0$, and since $a^2 + b^2 = \sqrt{3^2 + 4^2} = 5 = 1^2 + 2^2$, it follows that $(a,b) = \boxed{(1,2)}$.

Problem 2-2

Method I: Use an example. If $n = 12$, the remainder is 5 when we divide by 7. When we double, $2n = 24$, and the remainder upon division by 7 is $\boxed{3}$.

Method II: When the remainder upon division by 7 is 5, the remainder fraction is 5/7. Double to get 10/7, or 1 3/7. Hence, the remainder after doubling is 3.

Method III: Dividing n by 7, the remainder is 5. If we call the quotient q, then $n = 7q + 5$, and $2n = 14q + 10 = 7(2q+1) + 3 = 7k + 3$. It's easy to see that $2n$ is 3 more than a multiple of 7, so the remainder is 3.

Problem 2-3

The amateurs and apprentices work at the same rate, so the number of apprentices needed to complete the task in 1 day equals the number of amateurs needed to complete the task in 1 day. That number is $\boxed{12}$.

Problem 2-4

Method I: Since $\frac{1}{a} + \frac{1}{b} = \frac{a+b}{ab}$, let's evaluate $\frac{a+b}{ab}$. After clearing fractions in the original equation, we get $b(a+1) + a(b+1) = ab$. Expand the left side and combine like terms to get $a + b = -ab$. Finally, divide both sides by ab to get $\frac{a+b}{ab} = \boxed{-1}$.

Method II: Multiply by $(a+1)(b+1)$ and you will get $\frac{a+1}{a} + \frac{b+1}{b} = 1 + \frac{1}{a} + 1 + \frac{1}{b} = 1$; so $\frac{1}{a} + \frac{1}{b} = -1$.

Problem 2-5

In the diagram, surround the original square with a square whose sides are parallel to the axes, as shown. The y-coordinate of the upper vertex of the original square is 99, so each side of the new square is 99, and $x = 99$. The x-coordinate of the original square's upper vertex is 19; so the legs of the right triangles are 19 and 80, and $(x,y) = \boxed{(99,80)}$.

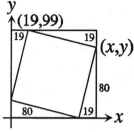

Problem 2-6

Among the integers from 1 through 60, there are 9 one-digit numbers and 51 two-digit numbers, for a total of $9 \times 1 + 51 \times 2 = 111$ digits. To make n as large as possible, begin with as many 9s as possible. From the integers from 1 to 49, delete all the digits except the five 9s. The number that then remains is 999 995 051 525 354 555 657 585 960. Now, we need to remove all but six of the digits to the right of the 9s on the extreme left. Leaving the last seven digits, the result is 999 997 585 960. That's a twelve-digit number, so remove one more digit, the 5 to the immediate right of the 7. Finally, $n = \boxed{99\,999\,785\,960}$.

Contests written and compiled by Steven R. Conrad & Daniel Flegler   © 1999 by Mathematics Leagues Inc.

Contest # 3   *Answers & Solutions*   1/11/00

Problem 3-1

Method I: Clear fractions to get $3a = 2b$. Square both sides and rearrange to get $9a^2 - 4b^2 = 0$. Multiply through by 100 to get $900a^2 - 400b^2 = \boxed{0}$.

Method II: If $a = 2$ and $b = 3$, then $900a^2 - 400b^2 = 900(4) - 400(9) = 0$.

Problem 3-2

Method I: The perimeter is 18, so the sum of the two dimensions is 9. Since each dimension is an integer, the possible dimensions are 4 and 5 (with area 20), 3 and 6 (with area 18), 2 and 7 (with area 14), or 1 and 8 (with area $\boxed{8}$).

Method I: In a rectangle with a fixed perimeter, the area decreases as the dimensions get further apart. The dimensions are positive integers, so each dimension is at least 1. The perimeter is 18, so the sum of the two dimensions is 9. The dimensions 1 and 8 are furthest apart, so the least possible area is 8.

Problem 3-3

To find the units' digit of the sum of the squares of some numbers, take the units' digits of the numbers, square these units' digits, add these squares, and use the units' digit of this sum instead. For example, the units' digit of $161^2 + 163^2 + 165^2 + 167^2 + 169^2$ is the same as the units' digit of $1^2 + 3^2 + 5^2 + 7^2 + 9^2 = 165$; so it's a 5. For any 5 consecutive odd integers, the sum of the squares of the units' digits is 165; and the units' digit of the sum is 5. Among the first 2000 odd positive integers are 400 groups of 5 consecutive odd integers. The units' digit of the sum of the squares of these numbers is the same as the units' digit of $400 \times 5 = 2000$; so the units' digit of the sum is $\boxed{0}$.

Problem 3-4

Method I: The probability that $x = y$ is $\frac{1}{9}$, so the probability that $x \neq y$ is $\frac{8}{9}$. Since x and y are chosen at random, it's equally likely that $x < y$ or $x > y$; so the probability that $x < y$ equals $\frac{1}{2} \times \frac{8}{9} = \boxed{\frac{4}{9}}$.

Method II: Just list the pairs. There are $9^2 = 81$ ordered pairs in all. The ones for which $x < y$ are:

$(1,2),(1,3),(1,4),\ldots,(1,9)$	8 pairs
$(2,3),(2,4),(2,5),\ldots,(2,9)$	7 pairs
$\vdots$	$\vdots$
$(8,9)$	1 pair

Since $1 + 2 + 3 + \ldots + 7 + 8 = 36$, the required probability is $36/81 = 4/9$.

Problem 3-5

Method I: We want the *largest* value of x, so let's try to find a positive value of x, not a negative one. For $0 < x < 1$, we know that $\frac{2}{x} > 2$. When $\frac{2}{x}$ attains its least integral value, x will attain its greatest possible value. The least integer greater than 2 is 3; and when $\frac{2}{x} = 3$, the value of x is $\boxed{\frac{2}{3}}$.

Method II: Let $\frac{2}{x} = n$, so $x = \frac{2}{n}$. As we did above in Method I, let's require that $0 < x < 1$; so $n > 2$. The least possible integral value of n is 3. This value of n yields the greatest value of x, which is $\frac{2}{3}$.

Problem 3-6

Place the figure on the coordinate axes, with the lower left-hand corner at (0,0). Let the length sought be r, and let the length of a side of the square be 2. By the Pythagorean Theorem, $(2 - r)^2 + (1 - r)^2 = (1 + r)^2$. Simplifying, $r^2 - 8r + 4 = 0$. Since $r < 2$, $r = \boxed{4 - 2\sqrt{3}}$.

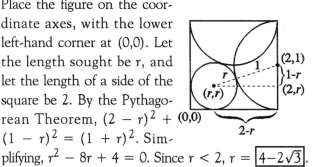

Contests written and compiled by Steven R. Conrad & Daniel Flegler   © 2000 by Mathematics Leagues Inc.

Problem 4-1

To form *any* list of 2000 consecutive odd numbers, add 2 to the smallest number 1999 times. For example, the list could be 1, 3, . . . , 3999. If the smallest listed number is n, then the greatest listed number is $n+3998$. The difference between the greatest and smallest listed numbers is $(n+3998)-(n) = \boxed{3998}$.

Problem 4-2

All three packages weigh 60 kg together, while the two lightest packages weigh 25 kg together. Subtracting, the weight of the heaviest package, in kg, is $60 - 25 = \boxed{35}$ or 35 kg.

Problem 4-3

Method I: The second right triangle is a reflection of the first, across the line $x = 5$. The vertex of the right angle of

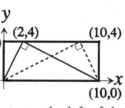

this second right triangle is 2 units to the left of the rectangle's upper right vertex, so $x = 10-2 = \boxed{8}$.

Method II: The product of the slopes of the perpendicular segments must be -1, so $\left(\frac{4}{x}\right)\left(\frac{4}{x-10}\right) = -1$. Thus, $x^2-10x+16 = (x-8)(x-2) = 0$, and $x = 2$ or 8.

Problem 4-4

Method I: Multiply every term of $-\frac{10}{3} \le x \le 1$ by 6 to get $-20 \le 6x \le 6$. Now add 7 to every term to get $-13 \le 6x+7 \le 13$. This is equivalent to $|6x+7| \le 13$, so we know that $(a,b,c) = \boxed{(6,7,13)}$.

Method II: Since $-c \le ax+b \le c$, it follows that $\frac{-c-b}{a} \le x \le \frac{c-b}{a}$. It's also true that $-\frac{10}{3} \le x \le 1$, so $\frac{c-b}{a} = 1$, and $c = a+b$. Substitute this into $\frac{-c-b}{a} = -\frac{10}{3}$ to get $\frac{a+b+b}{a} = \frac{10}{3}$, or $6b = 7a$. The smallest suitable value of a is 6, so $(a,b,c) = (6,7,13)$.

Problem 4-5

Since the squirrel ran at a fixed velocity[†] along the top of the log, the squirrel's actual path traced out a spiral on the log. This spiral looks just the way you'd expect a rope to look if it had been evenly and uniformly wound around the log. When

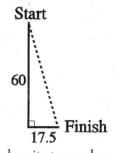

you "unwind" this rope from the log, its trace along the ground is a straight line. That trace, representing the squirrel's path, appears in the diagram as a dotted line. The log remained parallel to one side of the field, so in its final position, the log is one leg of a right triangle whose hypotenuse is the squirrel's path and whose other leg is the 60 m distance that the log rolled. [Note that the diameter of the log is irrelevant.] By the Pythagorean Theorem, the length of the path, in m, is $\boxed{62.5}$ or 62.5 m. [Note that the lengths of the sides of the right triangle are in the ratio 7:24:25.]

[†]Since velocity is a vector, direction and speed are both fixed whenever the velocity is fixed.

Problem 4-6

The sum of both roots of the quadratic equation $Ax^2+Bx+C = 0$ is $-B/A$. Similarly, the sum of all four roots of $Ax^4+Bx^3+Cx^2+Dx+E = 0$ is also $-B/A$. If the two real roots of the given equation are r_1 and r_2, then $r_1+r_2+a+bi+a-bi = r_1+r_2+2a = 14$. Since $2+5 = 7 < r_1+r_2 < 9 = 3+6$, it then follows that $7+2a < 14 < 9+2a$. Hence, $5/2 < a < 7/2$; and the integer nearest to a is $\boxed{3}$.

Contests written and compiled by Steven R. Conrad & Daniel Flegler   © 2000 by Mathematics Leagues Inc.

Problem 5-1

Since the area of the square is 64, each side of the square is 8, and the legs of $\triangle$I are 8 and 4. Since $\triangle$II $\cong$ $\triangle$I, the area of $\triangle$II is $\boxed{16}$.

Problem 5-2

We are told that $x = 15$ is a root, so we know that $15^2 - 5p(15) + 6p^2 = 0$. Expanding terms and dividing by 3, $2p^2 - 25p + 75 = (p-5)(2p-15) = 0$; so $p = \boxed{5}$.

Problem 5-3

We could list *all* primes under $200^{\dagger}$, but we seek a gap of 13 (or more) between primes, so let's list selected primes instead. For as long as possible, try to leave a gap of no more than 12 between listed primes. In the list 11, 23, 31, 41, 53, 61, 71, 79, 89, 97, 103, 113, the difference between two primes adjacent on the list never exceeds 12. Hence, the first of 13 consecutive composites exceeds 113. In fact, the next prime after 113 is 127. Here's why: 115, 117, 119, 121, 123, and 125 are respectively divisible by 5, 3, 7, 11, 3, and 5; so 114, 115, . . . , and 126 are all composite. The first of these 13 consecutive composites is $\boxed{114}$.

†One straightforward approach to identifying primes is to use the *Sieve of Eratosthenes*.

Problem 5-4

Method I: $(x^2 + x)^2 = 1^2 \Leftrightarrow x^4 + 2x^3 + x^2 = \boxed{1}$.

Method II: Since $x^2 + x - 1 = 0$, we have $x^2 = 1 - x$. Hence, $x^4 + 2x^3 + x^2 = (x^2)^2 + 2x^2(x) + x^2 = (1-x)^2 + 2(1-x)(x) + x^2 = 1 - 2x + x^2 + 2x - 2x^2 + x^2 = 1$.

Method III: Evaluate $x^4 + 2x^3 + x^2$ with a calculator, using either root of $x^2 + x - 1 = 0$ as the value of x.

Problem 5-5

Method I: $\cos 4\theta + 3\cos 2\theta + 2 = 2\cos^2 2\theta - 1 + 3\cos 2\theta + 2 = (2\cos 2\theta + 1)(\cos 2\theta + 1) = 0$. If the first factor is 0, then $\cos 2\theta = -0.5$, and $2\theta = 120° + 360k°$ or $240° + 360k°$, where k is an integer. Divide by 2 to get $\theta = 60° + 180k°$ or $120° + 180k°$. The solutions in our interval are 60°, $60° + 180° = 240°$, 120°, and $120° + 180° = 300°$. If the second factor is 0, then $\cos 2\theta = -1$, so $2\theta = 180° + 360k°$. Divide by 2 to get $\theta = 90° + 180k°$. The solutions in our interval are 90° and $90° + 180° = 270°$. The 6 solutions are: $\boxed{60°, 90°, 120°, 240°, 270°, 300°}$.

[**NOTE:** Since we asked for "degree-measures θ," the actual degree symbol is *not* required for full credit.]

Method II: If you use a TI-83, use degree MODE, let $y_1 = \cos 4\theta + 3\cos 2\theta + 2$, then ZOOM Trig. The intersections of y_1 with the x-axis include the solutions.

Problem 5-6

Method I: Use a pattern approach, but do not start with 2000 positive integers. Starting with 2 positive integers, the analogous sum is $(1+2) + (1 \times 2) = 5 = 3! - 1$. With 3 positive integers, the analogous sum is $(1+2+3) + (1 \times 2) + (1 \times 3) + (2 \times 3) + (1 \times 2 \times 3) = 23 = 4! - 1$. (Use mathematical induction if you want to write a formal proof that this pattern continues.)

Method II: If $g(x) = (x+1)(x+2)(x+3) \times ... \times (x+2000)$, then $g(x) = x^{2000} + f(1)x^{1999} + f(2)x^{1998} + ... + f(1999)x + f(2000)$. Setting $x = 1$, this last equation becomes $g(1) = 1 + f(1) + f(2) + ... + f(1999) + f(2000)$. But, if we set $x = 1$ in the first equation instead, then we'll get $g(1) = (2)(3)(4) \times ... \times (2001) = 2001!$ Equating these two expressions for $g(1)$, and rearranging terms, we see that $f(1) + f(2) + ... + f(1999) + f(2000) = \boxed{2001! - 1}$.

[**NOTE:** The relationship between the roots and the coefficients of a polynomial equation can be found in many precalculus textbooks, in the same section that the sum and the product of the roots is discussed.]

Problem 6-1

A 9×9 checkerboard pattern consists of 81 squares, of which 40 are of one color and $\boxed{41}$ are of the other.

Problem 6-2

Since $\pi \approx 3.14$, the first three factors on the left side of the given inequality are positive and the fourth is negative. The product of all five factors will be positive if and only if the fifth factor, n, is negative. Since $n < 0$, its largest possible integer value is $\boxed{-1}$.

Problem 6-3

If the books cost $\$x$ and $\$(40 - x)$, the problem tells us that $1.05x = 0.95(40 - x)$. Simplifying, $2x = 38$, so $x = 19$ and the dollar price of the cheaper book was $\boxed{19}$ or $19. [The $ symbol is optional.]

Problem 6-4

Method I: Multiply the first equation by 2 and subtract to get $y = \dfrac{1998}{1998-k}$, so $k \neq \boxed{1998}$.

Method II: The first line's slope is $-998/999$. The second line's slope is $-1996/k$. Unless they are parallel or coincident, two straight lines intersect in one point and have one common solution. When lines are parallel, they do not intersect and there is no common solution. These lines are parallel when $k = 1998$.

Problem 6-5

Method I: In $\triangle$I, $6^2 + (8-r)^2 = r^2$, so $r = 25/4$, $d = 25/2 = 12.5$, and $C = \boxed{12.5\pi}$.

Method II: $\triangle$II~$\triangle$III, so $8/6 = 6/x$, $x = 4.5$, and $C = 12.5\pi$.

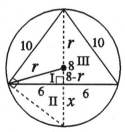

Method III: If two chords intersect in a circle, the product of the segments of one chord equals the product of the segments of the other. Thus, $(6)(6) = (8)(x)$, $x = 4.5$, and $C = 12.5\pi$.

Problem 6-6

The graph is known to be a hyperbola with vertical asymptote $x = 1/3$ and horizontal asymptote $y = -1/3$.

Method I: Look at the equation that results after shifting axes to coincide with the asymptotes, so that $\left(\frac{1}{3}, -\frac{1}{3}\right)$ is the origin of the translated coordinate system. Then (x,y) of the original coordinate system becomes (x',y') in the new coordinate system, where $x' = x - \frac{1}{3}$ and $y' = y + \frac{1}{3}$. For example, $(x,y) = \left(\frac{1}{3}, -\frac{1}{3}\right)$ in the original coordinate system becomes $(x',y') = (0,0)$ in the new coordinate system. Using the substitutions $x = x' + \frac{1}{3}$ and $y = y' - \frac{1}{3}$, we get $y' - \frac{1}{3} = \dfrac{x' + 1/3 - 3}{-3x'}$. Now, if we clear fractions and simplify, we'll get $x'y' = \boxed{\dfrac{8}{9}}$.

Method II: Using long division, $y = -\frac{1}{3} + \dfrac{8}{3(3x-1)}$; so $y + \frac{1}{3} = \dfrac{8}{9\left(x - \frac{1}{3}\right)}$, or $\left(x - \frac{1}{3}\right)\left(y + \frac{1}{3}\right) = \frac{8}{9}$.

Method III: Let $(x+a)(y+b) = k$. Then, $y(x+a) = k - bx - ab$, so $y = \dfrac{k - bx - ab}{x + a}$. But, $y = \dfrac{x-3}{1-3x} = \dfrac{-x/3 + 1}{-1/3 + x}$, so $\dfrac{-x/3 + 1}{-1/3 + x} = \dfrac{k - bx - ab}{x + a}$. Equate denominators to get $a = -\frac{1}{3}$. Thus, $\dfrac{-x/3 + 1}{-1/3 + x} = \dfrac{k - bx + b/3}{x - 1/3}$. Now equate numerators to get $k - bx + \frac{b}{3} = -\frac{x}{3} + 1$. Since the coefficients of x must be equal, $-bx = -\frac{x}{3}$, and $b = \frac{1}{3}$. Finally, $k - \frac{x}{3} + \frac{1}{9} = -\frac{x}{3} + 1$, so $k = \frac{8}{9}$.

Contests written and compiled by Steven R. Conrad & Daniel Flegler   © 2000 **by Mathematics Leagues Inc.**

Problem 1-1

Method I: Let's *guess and check*. Try the first three positive integers: 1, 2, 3. Their sum is 6. The product of the largest two is also 6, so the answer is $\boxed{1, 2, 3}$.

Method II: This solution shows that $\{1,2,3\}$ is the only set of three different positive integers whose sum equals the product of the largest two of them. Let the three different positive integers be x, y, z, with $x > y > z > 0$. Notice that this implies that $2x > y+z$. The problem tells us that $x+y+z = xy$, so $y+z = x(y-1)$. In this equation, if $y \geq 3$, then the right side would be at least $2x$, implying that $y+z \geq 2x$. But we showed earlier that $2x > y+z$. Thus, y cannot be ≥ 3, and the possible values of y are $y = 1$ or $y = 2$. Since $y = 1$ leaves no possible value of z, it must be that $y = 2$. Since $y > z$, $z = 1$. Finally, $x = 3$.

Problem 1-2

Rewrite the equation as $\frac{p^2}{14} = \frac{7n}{14}$. These fractions will be equal when $p^2 = 7n$. If $p = n = 7$, then $p^2 = 49 = 7 \times 7 = 7n$. Thus, $p = \boxed{7}$.

Problem 1-3

Let the length of a side of the square be $12x$. The dimensions of each rectangle are $3x$ and $4x$. By the Pythagorean Theorem, $(3x)^2 + (4x)^2 = 25$ and $x = 1$. The area of a square of side 12 is $12^2 = \boxed{144}$.

Problem 1-4

By trial and error, if $x = 3$ and $y = -1$, the value of $3x + 8y$ is $\boxed{1}$.

[NOTE: It is a theorem that, if the greatest common divisor of a and b is 1, then there always exist integers x and y for which $ax+by = 1$. Here, $a = 3$ and $b = 8$.]

Problem 1-5

Method I: $S = \left\{\frac{1}{15}, \frac{2}{15}, \frac{4}{15}, \frac{7}{15}, \frac{8}{15}, \frac{11}{15}, \frac{13}{15}, \frac{14}{15}, \dots, \frac{74}{15}\right\}$. The numerators of the first 8 terms are the whole numbers less than 15 that are divisible by neither 3 nor 5. The sum of these 8 fractions is 4, best obtained by the pairings $\left(\frac{1}{15} + \frac{14}{15}\right) + \left(\frac{2}{15} + \frac{13}{15}\right) + \left(\frac{4}{15} + \frac{11}{15}\right) + \left(\frac{7}{15} + \frac{8}{15}\right)$. To get the next 8 terms, just add 1 to each of the first 8. You'll get $1\frac{1}{15}, 1\frac{2}{15}, 1\frac{4}{15}, 1\frac{7}{15}, 1\frac{8}{15}, 1\frac{11}{15}, 1\frac{13}{15}$, and $1\frac{14}{15}$. Their sum is $8\times1+4$. The sum of all terms in S is $8\times0+4 + 8\times1+4 + 8\times2+4 + 8\times3+4 + 8\times4+4 = 8(0+1+2+3+4) + 5(4) = 80 + 20 = \boxed{100}$.

Method II: Whenever $\frac{n}{15}$ is in S, so is $\frac{75-n}{15}$, and each such pair has a sum of 5. How many pairs are there? The numerators are just those integers from 1 through 75 that are divisible by neither 3 nor 5. By the *Principle of Inclusion and Exclusion*, $\frac{75}{3} + \frac{75}{5} - \frac{75}{15} = 35$ of the first 75 natural numbers *cannot* be a numerator, so $75-35 = 40$ of them can be. Each of the 20 resulting pairs of fractions has a sum of 5.

[NOTE: The 40 actual numerators are: 1,2,4,7,8,11, 13,14,16,17,19,22,23,26,28,29,31,32,34,37,38,41,43, 44,46,47,49,52,53,56,58,59,61,62,64,67,68,71,73,74.]

Problem 1-6

Any factor common to two integers is always a factor of their sum as well. Since $2000 = 2^4 \times 5^3$, it follows that, as long as neither is even and neither is a multiple of 5, then the integers in each pair will have no common factor. Let the integers in a pair be n and $2000-n$. We need only consider n in the interval $1 \leq n \leq 1000$. Of these, 500 are even and 200 are multiples of 5. But, we already counted half of these 200, the multiples of 10, when we said that 500 were even. So, $500+100 = 600$ of the 1000 are discarded. The remaining pairs have a greatest common factor of 1. The number of such pairs is $\boxed{400}$.

Contests written and compiled by Steven R. Conrad & Daniel Flegler   ©2000 by Mathematics Leagues Inc.

Problem 2-1

Method I: The largest sum occurs when n is as small as possible. When $n = 1$, this sum is $\boxed{\dfrac{49}{36}}$.

Method II: Graph $y = \dfrac{1}{x^2} + \dfrac{1}{(x+1)^2} + \dfrac{1}{(x+2)^2}$. When $x = 1$, $y = 1.36111\ldots$, which is a larger value of y than for any other positive integral value of x.

Problem 2-2

Since $2^{3000} = (2^3)^{1000}$ and $3^{2000} = (3^2)^{1000}$, we need to compare only 2^3 and 3^2. Since $2^3 < 3^2$, the larger of 2^{3000} and 3^{2000} is $\boxed{3^{2000}}$.

Problem 2-3

$A = \pi r^2$ and $C = 2\pi r$, so $\pi r^2 + 2\pi r = 360\pi$. Since $r > 0$, $r^2 + 2r - 360 = (r-18)(r+20) = 0 \Leftrightarrow r = \boxed{18}$.

Problem 2-4

Any number that leaves a remainder of 10 when divided into 200 must be a factor of $200 - 10 = 190$. The prime factors of 190 are 2, 5, and 19. The smallest factor of 190 that's *greater than 10* is $\boxed{19}$.

Problem 2-5

Method I: Using the point-slope method, the steeper line's equation is $2x + y = 2a + b$, while the equation of the other line is $x + y = a + b$. Since the lines' y-intercepts are $2a + b$ and $a + b$ respectively, the base of the larger shaded triangle is $(2a+b) - (a+b) = a$. Similarly, since the x-intercepts are $a + b$ and $a + (b/2)$, the base of the smaller shaded tri-

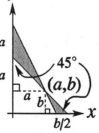

angle is $[a+b] - [a+(b/2)] = b/2$. Finally, the larger shaded triangle has (vertical) base a and (horizontal) altitude a, while the smaller one has (horizontal) base $b/2$ and (vertical) altitude b. The sum of the areas of these two shaded triangles is $\boxed{\dfrac{a^2}{2} + \dfrac{b^2}{4}}$.

Method II: In the diagram shown, the rectangle with one vertex at the origin has dimensions a and b. One of the lines through (a,b) has a slope of -1, so an isosceles right triangle with leg b lies to the right of the rectangle, and an isosceles right triangle with leg a lies atop the rectangle. Since the other line through (a,b) has slope -2, the smaller non-isosceles right triangle with one vertex at (a,b) has legs b and $b/2$. The larger non-isosceles right triangle with one vertex at (a,b) has legs a and $2a$. Finally, the larger shaded triangle has (vertical) base a and (horizontal) altitude a; the smaller one has (horizontal) base $b/2$ and (vertical) altitude b. The sum of the areas of these two shaded triangles is $\dfrac{a^2}{2} + \dfrac{b^2}{4}$.

Problem 2-6

Since there are two coats of paint, the region Watson painted in the morning could have been painted twice by Holmes in one hour. Thus, Holmes takes 30 minutes to paint this region once. Working alone, Holmes can finish one coat on the wall by lunchtime; so, 30 minutes before lunch, he could have painted everything except what Watson painted. Thus, Watson took 2 hours minus 30 minutes = 90 minutes to paint what Holmes can do in 30 minutes. Since Watson paints 600 m² per day, Holmes can paint 1800 m² per day, and the area of the wall is $\boxed{900}$ m².

Problem 3-1

$x^2 = x^4 \Leftrightarrow x^2 - x^4 = x^2(1-x)(1+x) = 0$, while $x = x^2 \Leftrightarrow x - x^2 = x(1-x) = 0$. The only value of x which works in the first equation but not the second is $x = \boxed{-1}$.

Problem 3-2

The smallest such positive integer is the least prime greater than 20. That prime is $\boxed{23}$.

Problem 3-3

If the diameter of each circle is d, then the height of the rectangle is d and its base is $3d$. By the Pythagorean Theorem, $(3d)^2 + d^2 = 20^2$, so $d^2 = 40$. Finally, the area of the rectangle is $(3d)(d) = 3d^2 = \boxed{120}$.

Problem 3-4

Method I: Drawing the diagonal as shown creates shaded triangles I and II in the diagram. Triangle I has (vertical) base 1 and (horizontal) altitude 2000, so its area is 1000. Triangle II has (horizontal) base 1 and

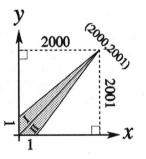

(vertical) altitude 2001, so its area is 1000.5 The quadrilateral's area is $1000 + 1000.5 = \boxed{2000.5}$.

Method II: To find the area of this quadrilateral, surround it with a rectangle, and then subtract the areas of the "excess" triangles. Using the diagram above, the surrounding rectangle has an area of $2000 \times 2001 = 4\,002\,000$. The sum of the areas of the right triangles is $(2000 \times 2000 \div 2) + (1999 \times 2001 \div 2) = 2\,000\,000 + 1\,999\,999.5 = 3\,999\,999.5$. Now subtract.

Problem 3-5

Since $1 + x^2 + y^2 + 2x + 2y + 2xy = 1 + x^2 + y^2$ simplifies to $x + y = -xy$, we'll use this simpler equation to solve for y, getting $y = \frac{-x}{1+x} = -1 + \frac{1}{x+1}$. Since x and y are integers, the denominator, $x + 1$, must be a divisor of the numerator, 1. The possibilities are $x + 1 = 1$ or $x + 1 = -1$. Thus, $x = 0$ or -2 and $(x,y) = \boxed{(0,0),\ (-2,-2)}$.

Problem 3-6

Sums of non-negative numbers may be rearranged in any order whatsoever without affecting the value of the sum. Rewrite the sum as $S = (\frac{1}{2^2} + \frac{1}{2^3} + \frac{1}{2^4} + \ldots) + (\frac{1}{3^2} + \frac{1}{3^3} + \frac{1}{3^4} + \ldots) + (\frac{1}{4^2} + \frac{1}{4^3} + \frac{1}{4^4} + \ldots) + \ldots$. Next we can use the formula for the sum of an infinite geometric series to write $S = \frac{1}{1 \times 2} + \frac{1}{2 \times 3} + \frac{1}{3 \times 4} + \ldots + \frac{1}{(m)(m+1)} + \ldots = (1 - \frac{1}{2}) + (\frac{1}{2} - \frac{1}{3}) + (\frac{1}{3} - \frac{1}{4}) + (\frac{1}{m} - \frac{1}{m+1}) + \ldots$. This is a *telescoping series* in which most terms subtract out. The sum of the series' first m terms is $1 - \frac{1}{m+1}$. Since m increases in size without bound, the value of S is $1 - 0 = \boxed{1}$.

Contests written and compiled by Steven R. Conrad & Daniel Flegler   © 2000 by **Mathematics Leagues Inc.**

Problem 4-1

Look for a pattern. The first term of the sequence is 12. The second term is the sum of the digits of $12^2 = 144$, and $1+4+4 = 9$. The third term is the sum of the digits of $9^2 = 81$, and $8+1 = 9$. Since every subsequent term is also a 9, the 2001st term is $\boxed{9}$.

Problem 4-2

Method I: Since $2^{10}+4^{10} = 2^{10}+2^{20} = 2^{10}(1+2^{10}) = (1024)(1025)$, the answer is $\boxed{1024}$.

Method II: First, $2^{10} + 4^{10} = 1024 + 1\,048\,576 = 1\,049\,600$. This is the product of two consecutive integers, so each integer is roughly equal to the square root of $1\,049\,600$. Since $1024 < \sqrt{1\,049\,600} < 1025$, the two integers are 1024 and 1025.

Problem 4-3

Let p = the Megalopolis population in 1987. Let t = the number of taxis in Megalopolis in 1987. The ratio of population to the number of taxis in 1987 was p/t. The current ratio is $1.10p/0.88t$. Increasing the current ratio's denominator by $0.22t$, would make the current ratio equal to $1.10p/1.10t = p/t$ = the ratio in 1987. We are asked to determine the per cent by which the present number of taxicabs should be increased to restore the ratio to its 1987 level. That per cent increase is $0.22/0.88 = \boxed{25 \text{ or } 25\%}$.

Problem 4-4

Method I: If $D = \begin{vmatrix} r & s \\ t & u \end{vmatrix} = ru-st$ has a negative value, then t and s must both be 1 (the probability of this is $\frac{1}{2} \times \frac{1}{2} = \frac{1}{4}$) *and* at least one of r, u must be 0 (the probability of this is $1-\frac{1}{4} = \frac{3}{4}$). The probability that both of these conditions occur is $\frac{1}{4} \times \frac{3}{4} = \boxed{\frac{3}{16}}$.

Method II: Of the $2^4 = 16$ different determinants, only $\begin{vmatrix} 0 & 1 \\ 1 & 0 \end{vmatrix}$, $\begin{vmatrix} 0 & 1 \\ 1 & 1 \end{vmatrix}$, and $\begin{vmatrix} 1 & 1 \\ 1 & 0 \end{vmatrix}$ are negative.

Problem 4-5

Method I: The point that is nearest to $(3,4)$ is the point of intersection of the circle $x^2+y^2 = 1$ and the line $y = \frac{4}{3}x$ [which is the line that connects $(0,0)$ to $(3,4)$]. This point has coordinates $\boxed{\left(\frac{3}{5}, \frac{4}{5}\right)}$.

Method II: In the diagram, which is not drawn to scale, label the sides of the larger triangle with a 3, a 4, and a 5. (This is not yet done in the diagram.) By similar triangles, $x/1 = 3/5$ and $y/1 = 4/5$.

Problem 4-6

Method I: In any circle, congruent chords have congruent arcs. Label each small arc a and each larger arc b. Then $3a+3b = 360°$, and $a+b = 120°$. Connect the upper left vertex to the lower left vertex. This new chord cuts off a 120° arc, creating a triangle with a 120° angle. By the law of cosines, the third side is $\sqrt{7}$. (Instead, you can extend the shortest side of the triangle, and drop an altitude from the opposite vertex. A 30°–60°–90° triangle and a new, larger right triangle are created. Use the Pythagorean Thm on the larger right triangle whose hypotenuse is the dotted line shown above). Now, draw a new circle with a 120° chord of length $\sqrt{7}$. Draw radii of length r to both endpoints of this chord, then drop an altitude from the center. Using the 30°–60°–90° triangle, we get $r = \sqrt{7/3}$, so $\pi r^2 = \boxed{7\pi/3} = 7.3303828583761842\ldots$.

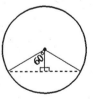

Method II: Use the law of cosines twice, once in each of the two triangles in the diagram. Each triangle has a 120° angle, so $x^2 = 1^2+2^2-2(1)(2)(\cos 120°) = 7$, and $x^2 = r^2+r^2-2r^2\cos 120° = 3r^2$; so $3r^2 = 7$, and $\pi r^2 = 7\pi/3$.

Contests written and compiled by Steven R. Conrad & Daniel Flegler

Problem 5-1

Expanding and combining terms, $(x+y)^2 + (x-y)^2 = 2x^2+2y^2 = 2(x^2+y^2) = 2(2000+2001) = \boxed{8002}$.

Problem 5-2

$$[2001] - [2000] = (1+3+\ldots+2001)-(2+4+\ldots+2000)$$
$$= 1+(3+\ldots+2001)-(2+4+\ldots+2000)$$
$$= 1+(3-2)+(5-4)+\ldots+(2001-2000)$$
$$= 1 + (1 + 1 + \ldots + 1)$$
$$= 1 + 1000$$
$$= \boxed{1001}.$$

Problem 5-3

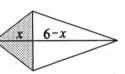

Since the shorter diagonal is a common base for both the shaded and unshaded triangles, the ratio of their areas equals the ratio of their altitudes. Hence $0.40 = \frac{2}{5} = \frac{x}{6-x}$, so $x = \boxed{\frac{12}{7}}$.

Problem 5-4

Method I: Let $\frac{2}{x} = a$ and $\frac{y}{3} = b$. We are told that $a+b = 3$ and $\frac{1}{a}+\frac{1}{b} = \frac{a+b}{ab} = \frac{3}{2}$. Since $a+b = 3$, it follows that $ab = 2$. The two solutions, obtained either by trial and error or by substitution and factoring, are $(a,b) = (2,1)$ or $(1,2)$. Finally, $(x,y) = \boxed{(1,3), (2,6)}$.

Method II: Clear fractions to get $xy = 3y-6$ and $xy = 9x-6$. Equating, $3y = 9x$, so $y = 3x$. Now substitute.

Problem 5-5

Method I: If x is the number and n is a non-negative integer, then $x = 10^n(\frac{1}{x})$. Since $x > 1$, $x = \sqrt{10^n}$. For the least such x, let $n = 1$; then $x = \boxed{\sqrt{10}}$.

Method II: Solve $\frac{1}{x} = \frac{x}{10}$ and see if there exists a solution greater than 1. That solution is $\sqrt{10}$.

Method III: Use base 10 logarithms. We require that $\log(1/x) = -\log x$ has the same mantissa as $\log x$. One possibility is that each mantissa is 0. But, if the mantissa of $\log x$ is m, then the mantissa of $-\log x$ is $1-m$. Thus, the only possible mantissas are 0 or 0.5. The least number greater than 1 for which this is true has a base 10 logarithm of 0.5. This number is $\sqrt{10}$.

Problem 5-6

If $z = x+yi$, then $z+1 = (x+1)+yi$. By DeMoivre's Theorem, both complex numbers lie on the unit circle centered at the origin of the complex plane. Note that $z+1$ is 1 unit to the right of z, horizontally. Hence, $x^2+y^2 = 1$ and $(x+1)^2+y^2 = 1$. When we subtract, we get $2x+1 = 0$, so $x = -\frac{1}{2}$ and $z = x+yi = \boxed{-\frac{1}{2} \pm \frac{\sqrt{3}}{2}i}$.

[**NOTE:** Since the radius of the unit circle is 1, and since $z+1$ is 1 unit to the right of z, the triangle connecting z, $z+1$, and the origin is equilateral and the angle between z and $z+1$ is 60°. Thus, n must be a multiple of 6. In fact, n can be any multiple of 6.]

Contests written and compiled by Steven R. Conrad & Daniel Flegler   ©2001 by Mathematics Leagues Inc.

Problem 6-1

The expression $\sqrt{3n}$ is an integer whenever n is 3 times a perfect square (that is, whenever $n = 3k^2$, where k is any integer). Since the problem requires that $k > 2$, let $k = 3$, from which $n = \boxed{27}$.

Problem 6-2

Rewriting, $\left(1+\frac{1}{n}\right)\left(1+\frac{1}{n+1}\right)\left(1+\frac{1}{n+2}\right)\left(1+\frac{1}{n+3}\right) = \left(\frac{n+1}{n}\right)\left(\frac{n+2}{n+1}\right)\left(\frac{n+3}{n+2}\right)\left(\frac{n+4}{n+3}\right) = \frac{n+4}{n} = \frac{51}{49}$. Solve this last equation to see that $n = \boxed{98}$.

Problem 6-3

100 centigrees = 360°, and $1° = \frac{100}{360} = \frac{5}{18}$ centigrees, so $54°54' = 54° + \left(\frac{54}{60}\right)° = 54° + \left(\frac{9}{10}\right)° = \left(\frac{549}{10}\right)° = \left(\frac{549}{10}\right)°\left(\frac{5}{18}\right)$ centigrees $= 15\frac{1}{4}$ centigrees $= 15$ centigrees $+ 2.5$ milligrees, so $(c,m) = \boxed{\left(15,\frac{5}{2}\right)}$.

Problem 6-4

Connect the three "dots" in the diagram to create a 30°-60°-90° triangle. The lengths of the sides of this triangle are $4\sqrt{3}$, 12, and $8\sqrt{3}$, and its area is $24\sqrt{3}$. To find the area of the shaded region, subtract the sum of the areas of the two circular sectors from the area of this triangle. Together, the sectors inside the triangle occupy $(30°+60°)/360° = 1/4$ of a circle. Since the radius of the circle is $4\sqrt{3}$, the area of the full circle is 48π, and the sum of the areas of the two sectors is 12π. Subtracting, the area of the shaded region is $\boxed{24\sqrt{3} - 12\pi}$.

Problem 6-5

Method I: The equations $\frac{a}{\sin A} = \frac{b}{\sin B} = \frac{c}{\sin C}$ follow from the law of sines. Therefore, $a = 16\sin A$, $b = 16\sin B$, and $c = 16\sin C$. Adding, $a+b+c = 16(\sin A + \sin B + \sin C) = 16\left(\frac{5}{2}\right) = \boxed{40}$.

Method II: $\sin A + \sin B + \sin C = \frac{a}{16} + \frac{b}{16} + \frac{c}{16} = \frac{5}{2}$, so $a+b+c = 16\left(\frac{5}{2}\right) = 40$.

Problem 6-6

Since $f(x) = x^2 - 3x + 4$ has a negative discriminant, f doesn't change sign. In fact, f is always positive, so if we multiply by f, we do not change the direction of the inequality. Thus, $x^2 - tx - 2 > -x^2 + 3x - 4$. Collecting terms, we see that $2x^2 - (t+3)x + 2 > 0$. This condition is true for *all* real values of x whenever the discriminant of the left side is a negative number. Finally, $(-t-3)^2 - 16 < 0 \Leftrightarrow t^2 + 6t - 7 < 0 \Leftrightarrow \boxed{-7 < t < 1}$.

Contests written and compiled by Steven R. Conrad & Daniel Flegler

Answers &
Difficulty Ratings
October, 1996 — March, 2001

Answers

1996-1997		1997-1998		1998-1999	
1-1.	8	1-1.	$-1, 0, 2$	1-1.	120
1-2.	-4	1-2.	28	1-2.	0, 3, 4, 5, 6
1-3.	16	1-3.	$\sqrt{433}$	1-3.	3
1-4.	-3	1-4.	1	1-4.	7
1-5.	103	1-5.	0	1-5.	-1998
1-6.	1989, 1995, 1998	1-6.	1013	1-6.	(1,3)
2-1.	8	2-1.	579 and 975	2-1.	5
2-2.	625	2-2.	18	2-2.	1998
2-3.	$\left(\frac{28}{13}, \frac{30}{13}\right)$	2-3.	3	2-3.	$\frac{1+\sqrt{5}}{2}$
2-4.	4096	2-4.	39	2-4.	18π
2-5.	33	2-5.	7	2-5.	$\{x \mid -\frac{7}{9} < x \le 1\} \cup \{x \mid x \ge 2\}$
2-6.	6	2-6.	36	2-6.	$(-7,0), (3,0)$
3-1.	3	3-1.	21	3-1.	13
3-2.	96	3-2.	12	3-2.	12
3-3.	$-\frac{4}{3}$	3-3.	288	3-3.	1
3-4.	48	3-4.	$\sqrt[3]{3}$	3-4.	666
3-5.	11	3-5.	27	3-5.	0, 3
3-6.	2:3	3-6.	$\frac{405}{26}$	3-6.	3 or 3 km/hr
4-1.	72	4-1.	(x,y), with x,y whole numbers for which $x + y = 98$	4-1.	20
4-2.	18	4-2.	25	4-2.	50
4-3.	$8\sqrt{3}$	4-3.	2½	4-3.	1
4-4.	2	4-4.	4	4-4.	$\sqrt{2} - 1$
4-5.	4	4-5.	$\left(\frac{2\sqrt{3}}{\sqrt{7}}, \frac{-6}{\sqrt{7}}\right)$	4-5.	$\frac{1}{4}$
4-6.	87531	4-6.	162	4-6.	1440
5-1.	160	5-1.	$0, \frac{26}{27}$	5-1.	2
5-2.	222	5-2.	13	5-2.	6
5-3.	-2	5-3.	$\frac{15}{64}$	5-3.	160
5-4.	Ali	5-4.	$\frac{2}{3}$	5-4.	$\frac{2}{10}$ or 0.2 or 1/5 or 20%
5-5.	30	5-5.	9.5	5-5.	6
5-6.	(2,17)	5-6.	$-x^3 + 10x$	5-6.	14
6-1.	-40	6-1.	-18	6-1.	1999
6-2.	5	6-2.	1997	6-2.	12
6-3.	48	6-3.	6	6-3.	24 or 24°
6-4.	0, 3	6-4.	22	6-4.	12
6-5.	$\frac{8}{9}$	6-5.	4π	6-5.	1
6-6.	3993	6-6.	3	6-6.	2916

Answers

1999-2000

1-1.	9
1-2.	118
1-3.	30
1-4.	15625
1-5.	8
1-6.	17

2-1.	(1,2)
2-2.	3
2-3.	12
2-4.	–1
2-5.	(99,80)
2-6.	99 999 785 960

3-1.	0
3-2.	8
3-3.	0
3-4.	$\frac{4}{9}$
3-5.	$\frac{2}{3}$
3-6.	$4 - 2\sqrt{3}$

4-1.	3998
4-2.	35
4-3.	8
4-4.	(6,7,13)
4-5.	62.5
4-6.	3

5-1.	16
5-2.	5
5-3.	114
5-4.	1
5-5.	60°, 90°, 120°, 240°, 270°, 300°
5-6.	2001! – 1

6-1.	41
6-2.	–1
6-3.	19
6-4.	1998
6-5.	12.5π
6-6.	$\frac{8}{9}$

2000-2001

1-1.	1, 2, 3
1-2.	7
1-3.	144
1-4.	1
1-5.	100
1-6.	400

2-1.	$\frac{49}{36}$
2-2.	3^{2000}
2-3.	18
2-4.	19
2-5.	$\frac{a^2}{2} + \frac{b^2}{4}$
2-6	900

3-1.	–1
3-2.	23
3-3.	120
3-4.	2000.5
3-5.	(0,0), (–2,–2)
3-6.	1

4-1.	9
4-2.	1024
4-3.	25 or 25%
4-4	$\frac{3}{16}$
4-5.	$\left(\frac{3}{5},\frac{4}{5}\right)$
4-6.	$7\pi/3$

5-1.	8002
5-2.	1001
5-3.	$\frac{12}{7}$
5-4.	(1,3), (2,6)
5-5.	$\sqrt{10}$
5-6.	$-\frac{1}{2} \pm \frac{\sqrt{3}}{2}i$

6-1.	27
6-2.	98
6-3.	$(15,\frac{5}{2})$
6-4.	$24\sqrt{3} - 12\pi$
6-5.	40
6-6.	$-7 < t < 1$

Difficulty Ratings

(% correct of 5 highest-scoring students from each participating school)

1996-1997		1997-1998		1998-1999		1999-2000		2000-2001	
1-1.	96%	1-1.	84%	1-1.	97%	1-1.	95%	1-1.	99%
1-2.	98%	1-2.	92%	1-2.	90%	1-2.	96%	1-2.	98%
1-3.	93%	1-3.	90%	1-3.	72%	1-3.	33%	1-3.	91%
1-4.	94%	1-4.	73%	1-4.	84%	1-4.	82%	1-4.	83%
1-5.	65%	1-5.	39%	1-5.	10%	1-5.	35%	1-5.	68%
1-6.	3½%	1-6.	½%	1-6.	50%	1-6.	56%	1-6.	41%
2-1.	90%	2-1.	91%	2-1.	68%	2-1.	96%	2-1.	92%
2-2.	78%	2-2.	90%	2-2.	91%	2-2.	98%	2-2.	95%
2-3.	77%	2-3.	72%	2-3.	87%	2-3.	98%	2-3.	89%
2-4.	79%	2-4.	94%	2-4.	80%	2-4.	43%	2-4.	86%
2-5.	49%	2-5.	26%	2-5.	13%	2-5.	71%	2-5.	26%
2-6.	21%	2-6.	35%	2-6.	8%	2-6.	20%	2-6.	½%
3-1.	90%	3-1.	93%	3-1.	96%	3-1.	99%	3-1.	98%
3-2.	91%	3-2.	98%	3-2.	90%	3-2.	95%	3-2.	84%
3-3.	81%	3-3.	94%	3-3.	74%	3-3.	79%	3-3.	62%
3-4.	68%	3-4.	71%	3-4.	71%	3-4.	66%	3-4.	58%
3-5.	27%	3-5.	11%	3-5.	75%	3-5.	71%	3-5.	53%
3-6.	41%	3-6.	18%	3-6.	33%	3-6.	6%	3-6.	60%
4-1.	96%	4-1.	98%	4-1.	94%	4-1.	87%	4-1.	99%
4-2.	97%	4-2.	82%	4-2.	77%	4-2.	96%	4-2.	97%
4-3.	71%	4-3.	90%	4-3.	83%	4-3.	91%	4-3.	75%
4-4.	60%	4-4.	62%	4-4.	72%	4-4.	35%	4-4.	70%
4-5.	52%	4-5.	24%	4-5.	76%	4-5.	62%	4-5.	62%
4-6.	23%	4-6.	73%	4-6.	33%	4-6.	43%	4-6.	5%
5-1.	92%	5-1.	90%	5-1.	82%	5-1.	97%	5-1.	94%
5-2.	91%	5-2.	88%	5-2.	70%	5-2.	92%	5-2.	77%
5-3.	46%	5-3.	26%	5-3.	81%	5-3.	43%	5-3.	70%
5-4.	84%	5-4.	74%	5-4.	33%	5-4.	35%	5-4.	81%
5-5.	65%	5-5.	70%	5-5.	34%	5-5.	48%	5-5.	23%
5-6.	12%	5-6.	10%	5-6.	44%	5-6.	4%	5-6.	4%
6-1.	95%	6-1.	75%	6-1.	96%	6-1.	97%	6-1.	96%
6-2.	71%	6-2.	93%	6-2.	88%	6-2.	93%	6-2.	93%
6-3.	90%	6-3.	82%	6-3.	54%	6-3.	90%	6-3.	42%
6-4.	65%	6-4.	59%	6-4.	79%	6-4.	62%	6-4.	38%
6-5.	18%	6-5.	80%	6-5.	90%	6-5.	41%	6-5.	27%
6-6.	46%	6-6.	44%	6-6.	31%	6-6.	10%	6-6.	16%

Math League Contest Books

4th Grade Through High School Levels

Written by Steven R. Conrad and Daniel Flegler, recipients of President Reagan's 1985 Presidential Awards for Excellence in Mathematics Teaching, each book provides you with problems from *regional* mathematics competitions.

- *Easy-to-use format designed for 30-minute time periods*
- *Problems range from straightforward to challenging*

Use the form below (or a copy) to order your books

Name _____

Address _____

City _____ State _____ Zip _____
                                      (or Province)   (or Postal Code)

Available Titles	# of Copies	Cost
Math Contests—Grades 4, 5, 6	($12.95 per book, $15.95 Canadian)	
Volume 1: 1979-80 through 1985-86	_____	_____
Volume 2: 1986-87 through 1990-91	_____	_____
Volume 3: 1991-92 through 1995-96	_____	_____
Volume 4: 1996-97 through 2000-01	_____	_____
Volume 5: 2001-02 through 2005-06	_____	_____
Math Contests—Grades 7 & 8‡	‡(Vols. 3, 4, & 5 include Algebra Course I)	
Volume 1: 1977-78 through 1981-82	_____	_____
Volume 2: 1982-83 through 1990-91	_____	_____
Volume 3: 1991-92 through 1995-96	_____	_____
Volume 4: 1996-97 through 2000-01	_____	_____
Volume 5: 2001-02 through 2005-06	_____	_____
Math Contests—High School		
Volume 1: 1977-78 through 1981-82	_____	_____
Volume 2: 1982-83 through 1990-91	_____	_____
Volume 3: 1991-92 through 1995-96	_____	_____
Volume 4: 1996-97 through 2000-01	_____	_____
Volume 5: 2001-02 through 2005-06	_____	_____
Shipping and Handling	$3 ($5 Canadian)	

Please allow 2-4 weeks for delivery

Total: $_____

☐ Check or Purchase Order Enclosed; **or**

☐ Visa / Dscvr / MC / Amex #_____

☐ Expires _____ Signature _____ Security Code _____

Mail your order with payment to:

Math League Press, P.O. Box 17, Tenafly, NJ 07670-0017
or order on the Web at www.mathleague.com

Phone: (201) 568-6328 • Fax: (201) 816-0125